Critical Guides to Spanish Texts

EDITED BY J. E. VAREY AND A. D. DEYERMOND

A Julio Ortega —
Con el recuerdo vivo
de un par de horas
miraflorinas sumamente
hospitalarias en
agosto de 1975.

Robert Brody
1/24/77
Austin

Critical Guides to Spanish Texts

16 Julio Cortázar: Rayuela

JULIO CORTAZAR

Rayuela

Robert Brody

Assistant Professor of Spanish, University of Texas (Austin)

Grant & Cutler Ltd *in association with*
Tamesis Books Ltd 1976

ISBN 0 7293 0014 5

Printed in England at
The Compton Press Ltd
for
GRANT & CUTLER LTD
11 BUCKINGHAM STREET, LONDON, W.C.2

Contents

Preface   7

1 The quest   9

2 Structures   37

3 Language and authenticity   56

4 Style and spontaneity   69

5 Conclusion   83

Select bibliography   86

for B. and Dana

Preface

The reaction of the general reading public and of critics to the publication of *Rayuela* in 1963 was extremely enthusiastic. Particularly interesting is the fact that this initial enthusiasm has continued unabated to the present day. In a recent article on Cortázar, Luis Leal suggests the preeminence of *Rayuela* not only in Cortázar's literary career, nor even merely within the confines of Spanish American fiction, but also in contemporary world literature (*3*, p. 409). Significant numbers of readers, writers, and critics seem to agree.

The following chapters present increasingly internal explorations of the resources of *Rayuela*. The method followed focuses on a division of the novel into its thematic (Chapter 1), structural (Chapter 2), linguistic (Chapter 3), and stylistic aspects (Chapter 4). My intention is not to exhaust the themes and the structural and stylistic means of expression, but rather to concentrate on focal points within each of these categories which I consider essential and/or particularly illuminating with regard to the novel as a whole. The brief concluding remarks (Chapter 5) summarize the main ideas established in the course of the analysis and attempt to show the interrelationships and unity in these ideas – that is, the shape of the whole formed by the parts: the vision of Julio Cortázar.

All page references to *Rayuela* are taken from the 17th edition (Buenos Aires: Editorial Sudamericana, 1974), though all editions after the second contain identical text and pagination. The italicized numerals in parentheses refer to the items in the Select Bibliography.

Thanks are due to the Bilingual Press for permission to use in Chapter 2 material published as "Twos and Threes in Cortázar's *Rayuela*" in *The Analysis of Hispanic Texts: Current Trends in Methodology* (First York College Colloquium; New York, 1976).

1 *The quest*

There is a steadily increasing number of articles and monographs on Julio Cortázar (see *1*). That this trend is due, in large part, to the appearance of *Rayuela* is obvious. This intense quest on the part of critics is a response not only to the body of Cortázar's work but also to *Rayuela* in particular, and even more specifically, seems to parallel the quest of Horacio Oliveira, *Rayuela*'s protagonist.

In order to set down the precise nature of this quest on the part of Oliveira-Cortázar (see *7* where Cortázar admits identification with his protagonist), we must first consider some general aspects of *Rayuela*. A fundamental consideration is its tone. If the reader had to select one adjective to describe Oliveira's state of mind, he would probably choose the word dissatisfied. Dissatisfied with what? With the human condition, it seems. This dissatisfaction establishes the predominant tone and forms the point of departure for the entire novel. Cortázar says that what he did in *Rayuela* was to respond to certain prevailing attitudes, feelings of frustration exhibited by youth which has had to live with

> . . . la sensación de que el mundo que sus padres les han ofrecido es un mundo que puede terminar en cualquier momento la bomba atómica y, realmente, eso no es ningún triunfo después de dos mil años de judeo-cristianismo, aristotelismo y platonismo. (7, p. 12)

Cortázar does not hesitate to theorize about the genesis of this poverty of the contemporary human condition (7, p. 12). Western civilization, in its formative period, that of the ancient Greek philosophers, seems to have gotten off the track at the outset with the appearance of the Platonic concept of dualism, the distinction between mind and matter, soul and body. He feels that this initial separation into opposites was false, and that its error has been compounded through the ages to such a point that today humankind is farther away from the experience of reality than it ever was precisely because twentieth-century man has inherited this dualistic tradition and culture.[1] It is helpful to recall that in what has been customarily understood as Platonism throughout the centuries, there were different values attributed to these paired opposites. The mind was superior to matter, as was reality to appearance, ideas to sensible objects, reason to sense perception. This concept eventually reached such an intense stage of development that scholars came to portray an entire century – the eighteenth – as an age characterized by the predominance of reason and the belief that the more mental energy expended on the powers of the intellect and the pursuit of the rational, the greater would be the good brought to mankind. The intuitive and the emotional were inferior categories; they constituted the opposite pole of the rational intellect. According to Cortázar, the Enlightenment and eighteenth-century rationalism inherited the dualistic tradition and continued to compound the basic error: the fragmentation, the false polarities and false values which have contributed to the present suffering state of Western civilization, marked by increased emphasis on technological advances and by an unwillingness to attempt to reverse the trend of spiritual deterioration.

What Cortázar does in *Rayuela*, then, is to express "en términos de novela lo que otros, los filósofos, se plantean en términos metafísicos. Es decir, las grandes interrogantes, las grandes preguntas" (7, p. 11). But this is just one of the tonic keys of the novel. Along with the metaphysical speculations which reflect the tone of dissatisfaction with the Western, Judeo-Christian tradition of Oliveira-Cortázar, there is also a constant preoccupation with language and literature (specifically with the

---

[1] Cortázar is not a philosopher. He does not present any systematic refutation of dualism in *Rayuela* or elsewhere. He does portray a character (Oliveira), nevertheless, who seeks self-fulfillment by trying unsuccessfully to shake off habits of thinking and living which he had acquired in accordance with a certain tradition. This tradition seems to be that of philosophical dualism. The reader interested in this philosophical tradition may find it traced from Plato through John Locke in Wilhelm Windelband, *A History of Philosophy*, 2 vols (New York: Macmillan, 1958), pp. 120, 130, 239 ff., 285 ff., 304 ff., 403 ff., 448. For an up-to-date treatment of these ideas in Cortázar within the context of modern philosophical concerns, see *10*, pp. 11-20.

novel) as vehicles for the transmission of the ideas which he feels
have contributed to the present sorry state of mankind.

> Lo que en *Rayuela* se dice . . . es que hasta que no hagamos una
> crítica profunda del lenguaje de la literatura no podremos
> plantearnos una crítica metafísica, más honda sobre la
> naturaleza humana. Tiene que ser una marcha paralela y, por
> así decirlo, simultánea. (7, p. 11)

So much for the general nature of Oliveira-Cortázar's dissatisfaction. The quest involved in *Rayuela* is a reflection of the
positive, creative facet of the dissatisfaction: the search for a
new world devoid of the false, artificial dualism referred to above
and the parallel search for new instruments (the novel, its form
and its language) to express this world. The following pages
represent an attempt to illuminate this parallel quest.

For an Authentic Reality

Horacio Oliveira, a disaffected Argentine intellectual on an
"extraordinary spiritual pilgrimage" (2, p. 212) to Paris in the
1950s, roams the city while sharing an apartment with La Maga,
a Uruguayan who cares for her infant son, Rocamadour, takes
voice lessons, and makes periodic visits to a seer. Oliveira, in his
forties, lives on a modest income provided by his brother, a lawyer
in Argentina, and spends his time pondering and discussing
"las grandes preguntas," listening to jazz records, and reading an
Italian novelist and literary theorist named Morelli with fellow-
members of a group constituting the Club de la Serpiente. While
living with La Maga, he has a brief affair with Pola, who subsequently contracts a fatal disease. La Maga and Oliveira part
company after the death of her child. Oliveira has a chance en-
counter with the writer, Morelli, who, from his hospital bed,
entrusts Oliveira and other members of the Club with a manu-
script of his work in progress. One night the Club members,
distressed by La Maga's misfortune and subsequent disappearance, suddenly turn against Oliveira for whatever unhappiness he
may have caused La Maga, and he finds himself forced to resign
from the Club. He is finally deported to Argentina after having
been found by the French police in a compromising situation –
inebriated and unzipped – with the clocharde, Emmanuèle.

In Buenos Aires Oliveira is reunited with Manuel Traveler, the friend of his youth who is now married to Talita, possessor of a degree in pharmacy and avid reader of encyclopedias. Oliveira moves in with an old flame, Gekrepten, across the street from Manú and Talita. He has a short-lived career as a door-to-door cloth salesman and subsequently takes a job with the same circus that employs Manú and Talita. When the circus owner decides to buy an insane asylum on the outskirts of the city, Oliveira, Traveler, and Talita decide to go to work for him there rather than stay on with the circus. Oliveira becomes obsessed with Talita's resemblance to La Maga. Traveler is bothered by this development, but not sufficiently to ask Oliveira to leave. Oliveira eventually becomes convinced that Traveler is trying to kill him and, with the aid of a patient, rigs his own room with a complicated network of string and strategically placed water basins and ball bearings. Talita, meanwhile, has told her husband about Oliveira's rapidly intensifying madness. Traveler enters Oliveira's room to find him tottering half-way out the window on the brink of suicide. At the end of the novel, Oliveira, surrounded by Manú and Talita, is being nursed back to health by Gekrepten.

The words, "¿Encontraría a la Maga?", which begin the first chapter of *Rayuela*, are significant since, in addition to their literal meaning, they also indicate one of the principal themes of the novel : a man's search for a greater intuitive, poetic dimension to his life (cf. *9, 10*). A fuller view of this theme requires, first, a look at the characterization of Oliveira and La Maga.

Oliveira arrives in Paris burdened by his "vagas tendencias intelectuales" which "se resolvían en meditaciones sin provecho . . ." (46). He is, in effect, "asphyxiated by intellectuality" (2, p. 223) and disillusioned by its negative results. Perhaps the most poignant example of this point, on a concrete, human level, occurs in one of the many wide-ranging discussions of the Club de la Serpiente. Oliveira, in a conversation with Babs, the potter, reflects upon a particularly obnoxious, myopic period of his youth :

– Todo es superficial, nena, todo es epi-dér-mico. Mirá, de muchacho yo me las agarraba con las viejas de la familia, hermanas y esas cosas, toda la basura genealógica, ¿sabés por

qué? Bueno, por un montón de pavadas, pero entre ellas porque
a las señoras cualquier fallecimiento, como dicen ellas,
cualquier crepación que ocurre en la cuadra es muchísimo más
importante que un frente de guerra, un terremoto que liquida
a diez mil tipos, cosas así. Uno es verdaderamente cretino, pero
cretino a un punto que no te podés imaginar, Babs, porque
para eso hay que haberse leído todo Platón, varios padres
de la iglesia, los clásicos sin que falte ni uno, y además saber
todo lo que hay que saber sobre todo lo cognoscible, y
exactamente en ese momento uno llega a un cretinismo tan
increíble que es capaz de agarrar a su pobre madre analfabeta
por la punta de la mañanita y enojarse porque la señora está
afligidísima a causa de la muerte del rusito de la esquina o de
la sobrina de la del tercero. (74)

This passage is not meant, however, to give the impression that
Oliveira has overcome his "cretinismo." Throughout the novel
Oliveira recognizes that "me costaba mucho menos pensar que
ser" (26). He constantly asks himself, "¿Por qué no aceptar lo
que estaba ocurriendo sin pretender explicarlo . . .?" (27). Oliveira
is reflective, introspective, with his "letras francesas en la punta
de la lengua" (160). Yet he feels sterile emotionally, lacks spiritual
vitality and the ability to communicate on a human level.

Y con tanta ciencia una inútil ansia de tener lástima de algo,
de que llueva aquí dentro, de que por fin empiece a llover, a
oler a tierra, a cosas vivas, sí, por fin a cosas vivas. (117)

La Maga, while not exactly the embodiment of "poetic instinct
in its pure form" (2, p. 223), as Harss suggests, represents, nevertheless, everything that Oliveira lacks. Where Oliveira is tortured
by his inability to "be," La Maga breathes freely the air of intuition. Her actions and reactions are based on spontaneity, emotion,
and empathy. Her mind is not cluttered by the sort of metaphysical anxiety which haunts Oliveira, who tells the reader at
one point "Fauconnier tenía razón, para gentes como ella el
misterio empezaba precisamente con la explicación" (41). Taken
out of context, this sentence would be open to diverse interpre-
tations. The reader of *Rayuela*, however, understands it as an
expression of delight on the part of Oliveira. He admires and even

envies La Maga, who relies on instinct instead of intellect and comes to decisions intuitively instead of dialectically.

La Maga's characteristic reliance on instinctive and intuitive behavior, independent of rational, intellectual considerations, takes on special significance for Oliveira for two reasons: (1) precisely because he himself is so completely devoid of these human qualities and (2) because he is ever conscious of this personal void and yearns to fill it. What is the nature of this special significance? The fact is that after examining Oliveira's relationship with La Maga (he unquestionably loves her but is not consciously aware of this love until after her disappearance), the reader becomes aware of a certain hierarchy established in the novel. On the surface, this hierarchy might seem to favor Oliveira. After all, is he not the more cultured, the more reflective, the better educated and, therefore, the wiser? The answer is a most emphatic NO! La Maga, in spite of her awkwardness and ignorance, the most conspicuous example of which is her inability to cope with motherhood, eventually resulting in the death of Rocamadour, still possesses a kind of wisdom superior to that of Oliveira. Cortázar implies that this wisdom takes the form of a profound authenticity and sincerity, candor, simplicity (in the best sense of the word) and a capacity for pity. All these are characteristics of La Maga and indicate what may only be termed a deep and genuine humanity. There are many examples in the novel to illustrate this point, one of which suffices since it is probably the best. In Chapter 20, shortly before La Maga and Oliveira split up, they have an argument. Oliveira is somewhat disgusted with the day-to-day living arrangements: he, La Maga, and Rocamadour all in the same room. La Maga, in turn, reacts by telling Oliveira to leave and not return. He responds with a characteristically aloof witticism, and then:

– Te tengo tanta lástima, Horacio.
– Ah, eso no. Despacito, ahí. (108)

Suddenly, Oliveira is hurt. La Maga has managed to penetrate his defenses. La Maga then confesses that she had been considering suicide by throwing herself into the Seine. Oliveira again responds coolly, mockingly: " – La desconocida del Sena [a short story by

Jules Supervielle] . . . Pero si vos nadás como un cisne" (109). La Maga again expresses her pity for him and finally admits to Oliveira that many things she had done for him – including going to bed with him shortly after their first meeting – were inspired by her acute sense of pity. Oliveira is stunned: " – Vamos – dijo Oliveira, mirándola sobresaltado" (109). Yes, La Maga continues, she had gone to bed with him because she recognized a certain danger Oliveira was in at the time. La Maga does not reveal the exact nature of this danger to the reader, but it is not really necessary. The reader knows, at this point in the novel, that Oliveira was suffering from a metaphysical malady: a steadily intensifying dehumanization, an inability to relate deeply to things and to human beings, a spiritual emptiness most clearly illustrated by his inability to feel pity for other human beings. The realization of La Maga's pity for him is shocking to Oliveira, for he recognizes her superiority to him. The characterization of Horacio Oliveira vis-à-vis La Maga becomes that of the poor-little-rich-boy, but on a cerebral rather than a materialistic level. All he has left as a human being are his metaphysical ruminations and, interesting as they are, they cannot take the place of a capacity for empathy with other human beings. He recognizes La Maga as a superior human being in this respect, and because of her superiority she acts as a mirror to Oliveira. When he comes into contact with her, he admires her for her "human" qualities but, at the same time, is reminded of his own failure as a human being. This explains the frequent reference in the novel to La Maga as Oliveira's "juez" and "testigo" (116 ff.).

La Maga's wisdom is revealed not only by her understanding of Oliveira and his dilemma, an understanding which frequently eludes Oliveira himself and occasionally the reader, but also by her intuitive capacity to foresee the outcome. After La Maga reveals that her pity for Oliveira was brought on by the dangerous state of mind she recognized in him, he patronizingly replies that the only danger he faces is of a metaphysical nature. La Maga responds:

¿Por qué decís: peligros metafísicos? También hay ríos metafísicos, Horacio. Vos te vas a tirar a uno de esos ríos. (109)

It is interesting to note that La Maga is the one with sufficient insight to come to the core of Oliveira's problem with one spontaneously invented metaphor. Though Oliveira does not immediately show appreciation for the prophetic nature of La Maga's declaration, he does acknowledge its accuracy a little further on in the novel. Oliveira reaches this conclusion by doing what he knows best. He calls to mind someone else's thought and analyzes it with great lucidity so that the reader sees a neat package whose contents (the original thought) belong to someone else (La Maga, in this case) but whose exterior wrapping (the lucidity of the analysis) is skillfully prepared by Oliveira. The following is an example of just such a package, seven pages after La Maga first coins the "ríos metafísicos" metaphor. Oliveira reflects:

> Hay ríos metafísicos, ella los nada como esa golondrina está nadando en el aire, girando alucinada en torno al campanario, dejándose caer para levantarse mejor con el impulso. Yo describo y defino y deseo esos ríos, ella los nada. Yo los busco, los encuentro, los miro desde el puente, ella los nada. (116)

An interesting feature of this reflection is its litany-like cadence generated by the anaphoric refrain, "ella los nada." After observing Oliveira's love, envy, and admiration of La Maga, the reader becomes aware of a new element at this point in the novel. We have already seen how La Maga might be considered superior to Oliveira as a human being. Now, however, Oliveira's thought just cited suggests almost an apotheosis of La Maga. Oliveira's lack of emotive power is due to his excessive penchant for introspection and reflection. This leads to his almost religious devotion to the intuitive, poetic spirit (the kind which characterizes La Maga).

Although the reader becomes aware of La Maga's eminent position at the top of the pedestal seen through the eyes of Oliveira-Cortázar, he never quite gets the idea that Cortázar intends La Maga to be representative of woman in general. Whereas Cortazar's two principal female personages, La Maga and Talita, are doubles and are held in equally high esteem by their creator, one has only to mention the other female characters in the novel – Babs, Berthe Trépat, Pola, Emmanuèle – in order to see the difference between the theme of the idealization of woman and Cortázar's vision of wanting to restore to its proper place alongside the contemplative faculties in human conscious-ness the intuitive, emotive spirit exemplified by La Maga. Never-theless, Cortázar, in his treatment of Oliveira and La Maga, projects what may be called a Romantic vision of the world in that he recognizes and condemns the loss of emotion and there-fore the sterility of a cold, cerebrally oriented universe. It is in this sense, also, that Cortázar may be termed not only a Neo-Romantic, but also an anti-intellectual novelist. He does not refute intellectuality but rather disputes its exclusive aura and the esteem, whose merit he doubts, in which it is held by Western civilization.[2]

The words which begin the novel, "¿Encontraría a la Maga?", are significant, then, because they reflect the quest theme which runs throughout the novel on many levels. The reader sees Oliveira in search of La Maga as the novel opens. Then, when he (the reader) becomes aware of the qualities and characteristics of Cortázar's enchanting female protagonist, he comes to under-stand that Oliveira's search for her transcends the primary level of a man looking for the woman he loves (though this primary level is real and not allegorical). His search for La Maga also suggests that broader, metaphysical quest of the contemporary intellectual who, aware of his error – exclusive reliance on cere-bral faculties – searches for a "vida sentida, creída,"[3] an essential

[2] Though allusions to Eastern philosophies and religions occur throughout *Rayuela*, Cortázar nowhere attempts to proclaim the superiority of Eastern culture to Western. See pp. 190–91 of *Rayuela* where Etienne indicates the falsity of both the "discursive base" of Western thought and the "intuitive base" of Eastern thought, seemingly because of their exclusive and segregated natures. As indicated in my following chapters, Cortázar's vision of life and literature has to do with fusion, not division. Eastern thought, particularly Zen (see 2), is but one of the many areas of philosophy emphasizing the importance of non-rational categories evoked in *Rayuela*. The attitudes suggested by Cortázar in *Rayuela* identify him as an admirer of modern Western "vitalist" trends of thought and literature (much of which is also associated with Romanticism and Neo-Romanticism) such as that of Nietzsche, Bachofen, Bergson, Keyserling, Klages, D. H. Lawrence, Unamuno, Robert Graves, and many others. It is interesting to note that both Oliveira and Gregorovius have read Klages (see pp. 190 and 507 of *Rayuela*).

[3] Julieta Fombona, "*Rayuela*," *Revista Nacional de Cultura*, No. 180 (1967), p. 80.

part of the new world sought by Oliveira-Cortázar in the novel.

This other-worldliness, in fact, is not only an essential theme in *Rayuela* but is also omnipresent in Cortázar's previous work. In his earlier work, the concept of "lo otro" took the form of purely aesthetic exercises which indicated the presence of the fantastic element beneath, behind, or beyond the common, everyday level of reality. This is especially true of the stories in *Bestiario*. In Cortázar's first novel, *Los premios*, there seemed to have been a hint of metaphysical speculation inherent in the fantastic ramblings of Persio, but the exact nature of this speculation is difficult to define owing to the abstruseness of his monologs. Only in *Rayuela* does Cortázar more fully develop his concept of "lo otro." It is now suitable to point out the dependence of the previously discussed theme, Oliveira's search for his intuitive self, upon the intimately related, broader theme of the quest for a new reality, a new world, a new frame of reference (see 9).

What precisely is this other reality mentioned so frequently in *Rayuela*? To answer this question, a previous one must first be posed. Is the theme of Oliveira's quest for his intuitive self as developed in *Rayuela* merely the novelistic treatment of a quest without the suggestion of a discovery, or does Cortázar indicate the success or failure of this quest? The answer is to be found in an examination of how Oliveira changes throughout the course of the novel. At the beginning of the novel we see him deeply troubled by his exclusively dialectical and distant approach to things and persons. But thanks to the influence of La Maga, he begins to change while in Paris. The reader witnesses this influence in his nascent feelings of pity for the ludicrous Berthe Trépat, even though the outcome of this "opening" proved in the end to be disastrous. And a conversation between La Maga and Gregorovius, just before she and Oliveira separate, provides explicit testimony of Oliveira's change.

> – Yo pensaba en Horacio – dijo Gregorovius – . Es curioso cómo ha ido cambiando Horacio en estos meses que lo conozco. Usted no se ha dado cuenta, me imagino, demasiado cerca y responsable de ese cambio. (160)

When La Maga presses Gregorovius to state how Oliveira has

changed, he refers to Oliveira's superior cultural background and keen intelligence. He continues:

> Horacio era bastante así, se le notaba demasiado. Me parece admirable que en tan poco tiempo haya cambiado de esa manera. Ahora está hecho un verdadero bruto, no hay más que mirarlo. Bueno, todavía no se ha vuelto bruto, pero hace lo que puede. (160–61)

So, even while still in Paris, Oliveira begins to change. Once in Buenos Aires, the change continues until it reaches its ultimate conclusion. Oliveira, more than ever influenced by La Maga when she is nowhere to be found, gradually rids himself of his spiritual problems but, in the process, is also divested of every trace of reason he formerly had – he goes mad. If in Paris the reader witnesses Oliveira disturbed by his inability to "be," his inability to approach people and situations and to react to them with a sufficient measure of human emotion and spontaneous intuition, the Buenos Aires episodes offer a complete reversal of this characteristic. From the moment Oliveira steps off the boat, he refuses to discuss with Traveler and Talita his life in Paris. This indicates not only his defensiveness, his reluctance to disclose the unusual set of circumstances which triggered his rather sudden return (the episode with the clocharde, Emmanuèle), but also reflects a changing Oliveira. Once in Buenos Aires, Oliveira no longer spends time in dialectical discussions about the nature of existence and reality, incapable of any sort of positive action since he would always intellectualize and come to realize the futility of any such action. Now the reader sees a different Oliveira. Instead of roaming the streets aimlessly searching for meaning in life, he is spurred to action, though within a rather limited realm. He works at a variety of jobs and writes when he finds time. In the Buenos Aires chapters he is, in turn, a door-to-door salesman, a circus employee, and an insane asylum attendant before succumbing to the occupational hazard of the latter. His approach to life is more natural and spontaneous. Gekrepten cares for his immediate, physical needs while Traveler and Talita provide him with a sort of spiritual paradigm which he envies in the same way he used to envy La Maga. In this second part of the novel Oliveira is endowed, as never before, with the kind of intuitive spirit already discussed. And being a more natural man, he is more spontaneous and child-like; he participates in all sorts of play activity, games, and humor. There was some of this in the Paris chapters (for example, the "glíglico" language La Maga and Oliveira used to speak), but it was limited and not representative, whereas in the second part of the novel, word games abound, as does a general spirit of play and humor and even hilarity. As a matter of fact, it is precisely this spontaneous, natural, intuitive spirit which catalyzes the serio-comic wooden board scene, one of the most unforgettable in the novel. Chapter 41 begins with Oliveira trying to straighten some bent nails, an insignificant and purposeless act. He is trying to straighten them simply because they are bent. When he finds himself incapable of straightening a single nail, he calls over to Traveler, who lives on the other side of the street, to throw him some straight nails and *yerba mate*. These spontaneous acts develop into the situation of Talita's mounting the boards in order to cross over to Oliveira's apartment with the nails and the *yerba*. All this is presented in a spirit of playfulness and naturalness.

If it were not for the danger involved in this episode, the reader would be led to believe that Oliveira had realized the object of his quest in this climactic scene: his intuitive self. Certainly what one observes in this scene is an Oliveira possessed of the intuitive qualities and spontaneity he was seeking throughout the first part of the novel, but dispossessed of his rational faculties. The change reaches its ultimate stages at the end of the Buenos Aires episodes. Whereas Oliveira was on the brink of madness when he was willing to risk a human life (Talita dangling in space), he becomes completely insane at the end of the novel when, convinced of Traveler's desire to kill him, he sets up an elaborate protective maze of string and ball bearings and threatens suicide. Oliveira's quest ends in failure, since he finds neither La Maga nor his "centro," "kibbutz del deseo," "absoluto," "reino milenario," all of which may be placed in the final Heaven section of the hopscotch design.

He does, however, manage to approach "lo otro," the other reality mentioned so frequently in the novel, which he had thought to discover by emulating some of La Maga's qualities. Constant reference to "lo otro" throughout the novel supplies the reader with ample clues both explicit and implicit as to its nature. But the references appear in such diverse situations and in such a variety of forms that a precisely focussed view of what constitutes "lo otro" seems to be lacking.[4] Certain structural characteristics of the novel, to be examined in detail in a later chapter, suggest a triangular quality of composition. On the most obvious level, the reader sees this in the basic division of the novel into three parts: the Paris setting, the Buenos Aires setting, and the "capítulos prescindibles." If one considers this arrangement on a visual basis, as a triptych, then he must also realize that the middle panel (in Buenos Aires) presents the most clearly focussed view of "lo otro" while the side panels present hints, allusions, explicit references – all of which offer only a partial, frequently blurred vision of the other reality sought by Oliveira and his creator.

In the first part of the novel, Oliveira roams Paris in search of otherness, "buscando siempre entrar" (50) in "esa otra oscuridad fabulosa" (61). He subconsciously has a presentiment of the other reality at the end of Chapter 13 when he says to one of the Club members: "Yo en realidad donde debería estar es jugando al truco con Traveler" (69). In many different ways throughout the novel, Cortázar expresses the need to search for new dimensions. He devotes Chapter 14 to Wong's torture photographs, then has Oliveira comment: "Lo que pasa es que me obstino en la inaudita idea de que el hombre ha sido creado para otra cosa" (73). In Gregorovius's words, "le duele el mundo"

---

[4] See Cortázar, "Para una poética," *La Torre*, No. 7 (julio-septiembre 1954), pp. 121–38. In this article Cortázar affirms the magical function of poetry by comparing the analogical method (A=B) practiced by the magician of primitive societies and the lyric poet of today. He also writes of otherness as that which remains outside of the human condition, whose essences the poet strives to possess in order to enrich his own being. Though Cortázar's remarks here help to illuminate his concept of "lo otro," it is not advisable to consider them as full explanations of "lo otro" as treated in *Rayuela*. A period of nine years separates the publication of the article from that of the novel. The article should be considered as a guide to the kind of completion, wholeness, and authenticity sought by *Rayuela*'s protagonist and creator.

(84). Later, referring to La Maga's poetic quality, Oliveira
reflects:

> Ese desorden que es su orden misterioso, esa bohemia del
> cuerpo y el alma que le abre de par en par las verdaderas
> puertas . . . Ah, dejame entrar, dejame ver algún día como ven
> tus ojos. (116)

At another point in the novel, he thinks that perhaps a woman's
love might be the key to what he is seeking, but quickly rejects
this idea: "Sí, quizá el amor, pero la *otherness* nos dura lo que
dura una mujer" (120). Besides, he concludes at the end of
Chapter 22, "La verdadera otredad hecha de delicados contactos,
de maravillosos ajustes con el mundo, no podía cumplirse desde
un solo término, a la mano tendida debía responder otra mano
desde el afuera, desde lo otro" (121). To sum up, then, in this
first section of *Rayuela*, Oliveira reveals the necessity and his
quest for another reality. He is not exactly sure what this reality
consists of, but he feels it to be of a "marvellous" nature and
imbued with La Maga's kind of spontaneity and intuitive force.

In the third section of the novel, the reader is afforded other
insights into the nature of "lo otro." Morelli writes:

> No podré renunciar jamás al sentimiento de que ahí, pegado a
> mi cara, entrelazado en mis dedos, hay como una deslumbrante
> explosión hacia la luz, irrupción de mí hacia lo otro o de lo
> otro en mí, algo infinitamente cristalino que podría cuajar y
> resolverse en luz total sin tiempo ni espacio. (413)

A bit further on, Morelli relates "lo otro" to a certain nostalgia
of lost innocence:

> ¿Qué es en el fondo esa historia de encontrar un reino
> milenario, un edén, un otro mundo? Todo lo que se escribe en
> estos tiempos y que vale la pena leer está orientado hacia la
> nostalgia . . . Detrás de todo eso [the obvious, the apparent, the
> superficial] . . . el Paraíso, el otro mundo, la inocencia hollada
> que oscuramente se busca llorando. . . . (432)

Along similar lines is Oliveira's suspicion that children, with their
natural reactions and the ceremonial, ritualistic aspect of their
games, experience the sought-for otherness (499). This otherness

is not some sort of esoteric experience; the other reality referred
to throughout the novel, is, in fact, a true and authentic reality,
not something to be discovered in the future but rather existing
in the present. Etienne tells us:

> ... la verdadera realidad que también llamamos Yonder ...
> esa verdadera realidad, repito, no es algo por venir, una meta,
> el último peldaño, el final de una evolución. No, es algo que
> ya está aquí, en nosotros. Se la siente, basta tener el valor de
> estirar la mano en la oscuridad. (508)

Morelli echoes this thought when he writes: "Sólo en sueños,
en la poesía, en el juego ... nos asomamos a veces a lo que fuimos
antes de ser esto que vaya a saber si somos" (523). Ceferino Piriz's
"La Luz de la Paz del Mundo" (Chapter 129) seems to be inclu-
ded in the novel to show how reason gone astray can completely
mask true reality with a ludicrous cover. An example of a
glimpse of an authentic reality is offered when Oliveira recalls
how La Maga would ask "por qué los árboles se abrigaban en
verano" (608). This is what Oliveira means when he mentions the
need for the resurgence of the "realidad poética" concept first
brought to the fore by the Surrealists and how this resurgence is
needed to place in its proper perspective the omnipotent "realidad
tecnológica" of the present (504).

The first section of the novel tells the reader of this marvellous
other reality, characterized by the spirit of La Maga. The third
section indicates that this other reality is the true reality (or, at
least, a satisfactory one because of its authenticity), with which
contact may be made by natural, authentic human beings (like
La Maga, Traveler, and Talita) who are spontaneous and even
child-like (the same characters plus the Oliveira of Part II).
Rational thought, if carried to extremes, will only blur and even
pervert ("realidad tecnológica," Ceferino Piriz's plan for world
peace) the vision of "lo otro," of the true reality (see *10*,
pp. 11–20).

This analysis of references to "lo otro" which appear so frequently in the first and third parts of the novel can only lead to
the conclusion that the true reality is approached in the second
section, in the Buenos Aires episodes. Regarding the so-called true
reality, Cortázar has said:

El problema central para el personaje de *Rayuela,* con el que yo me identifico en este caso, es que él tiene una visión que podríamos llamar maravillosa de la realidad. Maravillosa en el sentido de que él cree que la realidad cotidiana enmascara una segunda realidad que no es ni misteriosa, ni trascendente, ni teológica, sino que es profundamente humana pero que por esa serie de equivocaciones a que nos referíamos hace un momento ha quedado como enmascarada detrás de una realidad prefabricada con muchos años de cultura, una cultura en donde hay maravillas pero también hay profundas aberraciones, profundas tergiversaciones. (7, p. 11)

For it is only in the second part of the novel that Oliveira experiences a reality which his creator calls "profundamente humana." Oliveira experiences here a full range of human situations and emotions. Only in these chapters does he realize his love for La Maga, for example. He is also the object of Gekrepten's love. In this situation he is like an Odysseus welcomed home by a faithful but somewhat bovine Penelope. He also has the warm friendship of Traveler and Talita. This is a human relationship since Oliveira finds himself involved. He cares for them. There is emotive interaction in his human relationships. This was not the case in Paris, where he was mainly concerned about himself and his own problems, the chief of which was his inability to interact with people on a human level.

This is only a glimpse, however, of the aforementioned true reality because, ultimately, Oliveira is a failure. And his failure does not lack irony. In his intense desire to rid himself of his chronic tendency toward problematic introspection, he proceeds in a dualistic either/or manner. He becomes thoroughly and exclusively a creature of instinct, emotion, intuition, and spontaneity. He goes mad.

For an Authentic Literature

But just because Oliveira achieves a partial glimpse of otherness while in Buenos Aires, this does not suggest any sort of autochthonous message on Cortázar's part. Otherness may encompass spontaneity, intuitive behavior and humor to offset the poverty of the contemporary human condition, but *Rayuela* certainly does not promote the rather facile there's-no-place-like-home theme. Quite the contrary. Oliveira's spiritual quest also involves his desire to depart from everyday, fixed custom as a means of entering into a more authentic reality. Some examples will suffice to recall the constant and explicit references in the novel to these themes: custom and authenticity. Custom implies routine. Oliveira is incapable of accepting unchanging routine. At one point, between sleep and wakefulness, he complains: "*Estoy obligado a tolerar que el sol salga todos los días. Es monstruoso. Es inhumano*" (426). Morelli also writes of the necessity to depart from routine in order to seek new dimensions. On defining the nonconformist, for example, he says: "No es misántropo, pero sólo acepta de hombres y mujeres la parte que no ha sido plastificada por la superestructura social" (442). Oliveira shares this view of custom as petrification:

> Imagino al hombre como una ameba que tira seudópodos para alcanzar y envolver su alimento. Hay seudópodos largos y cortos, movimientos, rodeos. Un día eso *se fija* (lo que llaman la madurez, el hombre hecho y derecho). (463)

This view is expressed in many different circumstances, even when the Club members listen to jazz. At one point, while listening to records from Louis Armstrong's authentic period, that is, before custom ruined him, Oliveira says: "Lo que sigue es costumbre y papel carbónico . . . y Satchmo . . . cansado y monetizado y sin importarle un pito lo que hace, pura rutina . . ." (68).

The references to authenticity in the novel are also varied and multiform. Sometimes they are contained in the thoughts of other writers cited by Cortázar. Lezama Lima, for example, is quoted as saying: "Procuremos inventar pasiones nuevas, o reproducir las viejas con pareja intensidad" (457). And Pauwels and Bergier, commenting on the failure of customary approaches to the nature of knowledge (dualistic thought), say: "¿Pero qué decir de la insuficiencia de la inteligencia binaria en sí misma? La existencia interna, la esencia de las cosas se le escapa" (466). Oliveira goes on to suggest that the essence of things (authenticity) may be experienced only by a destruction of dualistic categories and a willingness to accept other dimensions. One such dimension is illustrated below; it involves the illogical fusion of differences, both spatial and temporal:

> El verdadero sueño se situaba en una zona imprecisa, del lado del despertar pero sin que él estuviera verdaderamente despierto; para hablar de eso hubiera sido necesario valerse de otras referencias, eliminar esos rotundos *soñar* y *despertar* que no querían decir nada, situarse más bien en esa zona donde otra vez se proponía la casa de la infancia, la sala y el jardín en un presente nítido. . . . Pero en el sueño, la sala con las dos ventanas que daban al jardín era a la vez la pieza de la Maga; el olvidado pueblo bonaerense y la rue du Sommerard se aliaban sin violencia, no yuxtapuestos ni imbricados sino fundidos, y en la contradicción abolida sin esfuerzo había la sensación de estar en lo propio, en lo esencial. . . . (555)

To sum up, one may equate custom with blind obedience to logical, accepted categories such as chronologically ordered time and logical assimilations in space. Also, from a look at the above examples it is clear what Cortázar's attitude is toward custom vis-à-vis authenticity. In order to experience authenticity, it is necessary to depart from custom and habit whenever it becomes petrified. The time-space fusions, as in the last example cited above, represent one of these departures.[5]

As the reader will see below, all this is highly pertinent to a discussion of the literary themes in *Rayuela*. *Rayuela* is certainly not the first novel to treat itself as one of the principal themes. The *Quijote* of 1615 begins on that very note. And since the entire concept of literature plays such an important role in *Rayuela*, an analysis is necessary.

Cortázar's ideas about literature in general and the novel in particular are set forth mainly by Morelli. Needless to say, those readers who elect the first of the two methods of reading *Rayuela* suggested by Cortázar will not be exposed to these ideas, since

[5] This fusion of two different times and two different places—present and past, Paris and Buenos Aires—is illogical. It is necessary to clarify, however, that Cortázar does not equate habit with logic (negative) and authenticity with illogicality (positive). Rather, he seems to defend the concepts of fluidity and flexibility as opposed to solidarity and rigidity (see *4*, pp. 69–84 for further comments on this "fluid" aspect of *Rayuela*).

Morelli's thoughts are set down in the "De otros lados (*Capítulos prescindibles*)" section. Morelli, however, is not the only person-age to show his concern with literature. Oliveira, sometimes as personage and other times as narrator, also expresses his opinions, as do the members of the Club de la Serpiente. I shall have more to say about this matter below when I discuss the role of the reader.

Previously, I dealt with Oliveira's dissatisfaction with himself and the human condition and his quest for another reality. The author's preoccupation with literature is an integral part of this critique and this quest. The literary quest, then, is just as import-ant as the metaphysical one. Let us recall Cortázar's words: "Tiene que ser una marcha paralela y, por así decirlo, simultánea." Morelli echoes this thought when, writing about absolutes, he says:

> Sólo hay una belleza que todavía puede darme ese acceso [to an absolute and satisfactory reality] : aquella que es un fin y no un medio, y lo es porque su creador ha identificado en sí mismo su sentido de la condición humana con su sentido de la condición de artista. (539)

And, as a literary artist, Morelli proposes "una destrucción de formas (de fórmulas) literarias" (491) in order to recover "el uso original de la palabra" (540). But this is still somewhat vague. Just who is Morelli and what does he hope to accomplish by attempting to destroy literary forms?

He is a personage in *Rayuela* who is a novelist, literary theorist, and "active" reader. As such he may be said to represent an alter ego of Cortázar. Just as Oliveira may be seen as a personage whose metaphysical preoccupations reflect those of his creator, Morelli's ideas about literature and the novel clearly reflect Cortázar's own – in this sense, then, he is a literary double. This becomes apparent not only from a comparison of Morelli's literary theories in themselves with those of Cortázar (see 2 and 7), but also from an examination of the autobiographical references con-tained in his statements. For example, Morelli speaks of the rotting of his prose, but in terms of a progression from impurity to purity (488). At another point, Oliveira reveals Morelli's feel-

ings about purely aesthetic literary criteria: "Morelli entiende
que el mero escribir estético es un escamoteo y una mentira . . ."
(500). Similarly, we are told:

> [Morelli] Se iba alejando así cada vez más de la utilización
> profesional de la literatura, de ese tipo de cuentos o poemas que
> le habían valido su prestigio inicial. (501)

These are all statements that Cortázar has made about his own
work. With this in mind, let us now proceed to a fuller examination of the literary ideas expressed in the novel.

First, it is fitting to mention that Morelli's literary theories are
not set down in a systematic, organized manner. They are scattered throughout the last third of the novel, usually (but not
always) under the chapter heading *Morelliana*. The general
direction of Morelli's statements is revealed in Chapter 73,
actually the first chapter for those "active" readers who select the
second way of reading the novel. The narrator (probably Oliveira)
speaks of the use of literature for the invention of a new world
(438–39). But Morelli tells us that this invention is to be realized
by a subtraction from rather than an addition to:

> Si el volumen o el tono de la obra pueden llevar a creer que
> el autor intentó una suma, apresurarse a señalarle que está ante
> la tentativa contraria, la de una *resta* implacable. (595)

The subtraction of what? Occasionally logic, so that the appearance of absurdity in literature will not be uncommon. This means
a denial of psychological literature, that is, literature which deals
principally with cause-and-effect situations and characterizations
(497). What this amounts to, then, writes Morelli, is "una repulsa
de la literatura; repulsa parcial puesto que se apoya en la palabra,
pero que debe velar en cada operación que emprendan autor y
lector" (452). He proposes an anti-literature,[6] but this in itself is
not just a negative force. After all, his negative proposals find
expression from the point of view of literature itself (*Rayuela*).

---

[6] The Cervantine example is apparent here. See especially José F. Montesinos,
"Cervantes antinovelista," *Nueva Revista de Filología Hispánica*, VII (1953),
499–514. See also Edna Coll, "Aspectos cervantinos en Julio Cortázar," *Revista
Hispánica Moderna*, XXXIV (1968), 596–604 and, in the same number, María
Teresa Babín, "La antinovela en Hispanoamérica," 523–32.

The Club members themselves question the validity of Morelli's revolution. When Oliveira suggests that Morelli's ideas may be merely negative, without any constructive qualities, Etienne disagrees by stating that Morelli's attack on literature suffices as a first step (505). Etienne goes on to say that the essence of this first step is to break the reader's mental habits and "echar abajo las formas usuales, cosa corriente en todo buen artista" (505).

Now we can see more clearly the relationship between Morelli's literary ideas and the concepts of custom and habit outlined above. The Club characterizes Morelli's narrative technique as "una incitación a salirse de las huellas" (508). But could this not be more effectively accomplished by a clearly expressed and systematic exposition of ideas rather than a loose, scattered non-arrangement of *Morelliana*? Definitely not. According to Morelli, "no se puede denunciar nada si se lo hace dentro del sistema al que pertenece lo denunciado" (509). Ronald offers perhaps the best summary of what Morelli is trying to accomplish. He says that in this predominantly technological world, Morelli wants to save something that is dying, "pero para salvarlo hay que matarlo antes o por lo menos hacerle tal transfusión de sangre que sea como una resurrección" (506). This clearly seems to reflect a desire to restore an authentic, enduring, poetic reality (cf. pp. 504 ff.) – in short, an authentic literature.

What about the novel in particular? Morelli indicates that there have been too many novelists practicing the passive role of the *voyeur*. It is necessary, he says, for the novelist to be a *voyant*, to take a more active role in his creation (544). Similarly, the novelist has relied too much on descriptive techniques: ". . . basta de técnicas puramente descriptivas, de novelas 'del comportamiento'" (544). What is necessary is a basic change in the novelist's conception of his personages. Morelli does acknowledge the changes in form that have occurred in the novel, but he considers these changes merely external and superficial:

Las formas exteriores de la novela han cambiado, pero sus héroes siguen siendo los avatares de Tristán, de Jane Eyre, de Lafcadio, de Leopold Bloom, gente de la calle, de la casa, de la alcoba, *caracteres*. (497)

The novelist should place the situation (the circumstances) in the personage and not vice versa. In this manner, personages would become persons, and then: "hay como una extrapolación mediante la cual ellos saltan hacia nosotros, o nosotros hacia ellos" (543). Furthermore, the aspect of Cortázar's vision which calls for the necessity of a new man to make a new world is expressed by Morelli in terms of an anthropophany (that is, appearance of the human). The element of humor is both cause (partial) and characteristic of this anthropophany. Morelli writes: "Intentar el 'roman comique' en el sentido en que un texto alcance a insinuar otros valores y colabore así en esa antropofanía que seguimos creyendo posible" (452).

Finally, in the same way as we saw Morelli advocating an anti-literature, he declares the necessity for an anti-novel as a means of breaking with closed-order custom and habit, characteristic of the traditional novel. In the passage below, Morelli discloses that he is not fanatical in his quest for the anti-novel:

Provocar, asumir un texto desaliñado, desanudado, incongruente, minuciosamente antinovelístico (aunque no anti-novelesco). Sin vedarse los grandes efectos del género cuando la situación lo requiera, pero recordando el consejo gidiano, *ne jamais profiter de l'élan acquis*. Como todas las criaturas de elección del Occidente, la novela se contenta con un orden cerrado. Resueltamente en contra, buscar también aquí la apertura y para eso cortar de raíz toda construcción sistemática de caracteres y situaciones. Método: la ironía, la autocrítica incesante, la incongruencia, la imaginación al servicio de nadie. (452)

He also makes an analogy between the anti-novel he is proposing and certain characteristics of Zen philosophy. The analogous element is that both Morelli's anti-novel and certain Zen techniques seek other orders, dimensions, openings:

. . . cuanto más violenta fuera la contradicción interna, más eficacia podría dar a una, digamos, técnica al modo Zen. A cambio del bastonazo en la cabeza, una novela absolutamente antinovelesca, con el escándalo y el choque consiguiente, y quizá con una apertura para los más avisados. (490)

As we shall see below, "los más avisados" refer to certain kinds of readers. But before proceeding to a discussion of the role of the reader, let us examine one final aspect of Morelli's anti-novel. He says it must not bear messages; rather his anti-novel is to be a coagulant and catalyst:

> Tomar de la literatura eso que es puente vivo de hombre a hombre, y que el tratado o el ensayo sólo permite entre especialistas. Una narrativa que no sea pretexto para la trasmisión de un 'mensaje' (no hay mensaje, hay mensajeros y eso es el mensaje, así como el amor es el que ama); una narrativa que actúe como coagulante de vivencias, como catalizadora de nociones confusas y mal entendidas, y que incida en primer término en el que la escribe, para lo cual hay que escribirla como antinovela porque todo orden cerrado dejará sistemáticamente afuera esos anuncios que pueden volvernos mensajeros, acercarnos a nuestros propios límites de los que tan lejos estamos cara a cara. (453)

It is now necessary to examine the role of the reader according to Morelli's ideas on literature and the novel. The many references in *Rayuela* to the importance of the reader are at once the most provocative and the most disappointing aspects of Cortázar's literary ideas. On the provocative side, there is in *Rayuela* not only an interaction but a constant shifting of roles between novelist, personage, reader, and/or critic. This adds new elements of dynamism and dimension to the novel. The disappointing aspect is that Cortázar seems to suggest that extra-literary effects are necessary in order to gain a fuller comprehension of the novel, all of which tends to reduce rather than extend and intensify the significance of literature.

Morelli writes that while refusing to write literature of a psychological, cause-and-effect nature, he also, at the same time, wants to put a certain reader into a personal world devoid of such things as causal articulation, characteristic of the "psychological novel" (497). Why? What importance does the reader hold for Morelli? He tells us unequivocally that the reader is his main concern:

> Por lo que me toca, me pregunto si alguna vez conseguiré hacer sentir que el verdadero y único personaje que me interesa

es el lector, en la medida en que algo de lo que escribo debería
contribuir a mutarlo, a desplazarlo, a extrañarlo, a enajenarlo.
(497-98)

But this does not apply for just any reader at all, not even for the
average reader. Rather, says Morelli, "hay solamente esperanza de
un cierto diálogo con un cierto y remoto lector" (539).

This now brings us to Morelli-Cortázar's distinction between
the *lector-hembra* and the *lector-cómplice*. In general terms, the
former (who does not have to be a female) is the passive, easily
satisfied reader while the latter is the active, demanding reader.
Synonymous with the *lector-hembra* is the *lector-alondra*. Morelli
describes in derogatory terms his former prose style as "un espejo
para lectores-alondra; se miraban, se solazaban, se reconocían
. . ." (539). So it is with the *lector-hembra*. Morelli advocates
demotic writing for this reader (452), who contents himself with
nothing more problematic than pretty façades (454). But it is
Oliveira who gives us perhaps the best definition of the *lector-
hembra*. Speaking about Morelli's work, Oliveira interprets
Morelli as one who understands that "el mero escribir estético es
un escamoteo y una mentira . . ." (500). The autobiographical
reference here is clear. Cortázar has expressed the same idea
many times about his own work. This mere aesthetic writing,
says Oliveira,

> . . . acaba por suscitar al lector-hembra, al tipo que no quiere
> problemas sino soluciones, o falsos problemas ajenos que le
> permiten sufrir cómodamente sentado en su sillón, sin
> comprometerse en el drama que también debería ser el suyo.
> (500)

Needless to say, it is not the *lector-hembra* whom Morelli is
trying to reach; it is the active reader, the *lector-cómplice*, who
interests him. What kind of text to produce for this kind of
reader? One which would oblige him to be an accomplice, "al
murmurarle, por debajo del desarrollo convencional, otros rumbos
más esotéricos" (452). This kind of reader must be active in that,
far from being satisfied with a mere façade as would the *lector-
hembra*, he feels compelled to penetrate the doors and windows
in order to search for the mystery beyond the façade. This
constitutes a complicity with the novelist. Morelli says:

Mejor, le da como una fachada, con puertas y ventanas detrás de las cuales se está operando un misterio que el lector cómplice deberá buscar (de ahí la complicidad) y quizá no encontrará (de ahí el copadecimiento). (454)

This leads us to a consideration of Morelli's most interesting statement about the situation of the reader. Parenthetically, it should be clear that when Morelli speaks of his concern for the reader, he means the *lector-cómplice*, unless he states otherwise. Let us call to mind again the passage where he states in no uncertain terms that the only personage who interests him is the reader, "en la medida en que algo de lo que escribo debería contribuir a mutarlo, a desplazarlo, a extrañarlo, a enajenarlo" (497–98). In a sense he explains this statement when, upon writing about the situation of the reader, he says that every novelist hopes that his reader will understand him. He (the reader) may accomplish this by either participating in his own experience (which would necessarily have to be similar to the novelist's) or by picking up a given message in the novel and incarnating it (453). Morelli then goes on to suggest the idea of the simultaneity of the *lector-cómplice*:

El novelista romántico quiere ser comprendido por sí mismo o a través de sus héroes; el novelista clásico quiere enseñar, dejar una huella en el camino de la historia.

Posibilidad tercera: la de hacer del lector un cómplice, un camarada de camino. Simultaneizarlo, puesto que la lectura abolirá el tiempo del lector y lo trasladará al del autor. Así el lector podría llegar a ser copartícipe y copadeciente de la experiencia por la que pasa el novelista, *en el mismo momento y en la misma forma.* (453).

Until now I have dealt with the theory, the ideas about literature, the novel, and the reader which are expressed in *Rayuela.* The next facet to be considered is the *praxis.* Are these theoretical ideas actually put into practice in the main body of the narrative ("Del lado de allá," "Del lado de acá")? And if Cortázar the novelist does put into practice the ideas of Morelli the theorist, to what extent and in what manner is this realized?

A convenient starting point is the topic just discussed: the situation of the reader. Recall that at the outset of this discussion, I indicated that one dimension of an authentic reality, for Oliveira, involved certain illogical spatial-temporal fusions. Oliveira's room in his childhood home in Buenos Aires became one and the same as La Maga's room in Paris. Morelli, in the passage above, expresses a similar concept (illogical, irrational fusion) when he speaks of making the reader an accomplice by making his reality simultaneous with that of the novelist. This parallelism of concepts, Oliveira on the one hand (the metaphysical) and Morelli on the other (the literary), helps to explain Morelli's previously cited statement about the creator of beauty who identifies his sense of the human condition with his sense of his own condition as an artist.

I began this discussion of the reader's role by saying that this particular theme was both provocative and disappointing. It is provocative in that Cortázar, in his novel, goes beyond the level of mere theory. What are Oliveira and the other members of the Club de la Serpiente if not accomplice-readers? With the exception, of course, of La Maga who is the *lector-hembra por excelencia*. Morelli gives them the key to his apartment so they can read and put his notes in order. They read, annotate, and discuss his writings in frequent meetings. The element of simultaneity occurs when, in Morelliana chapters, we realize that we, as persons, and the Club members, as personages, are reading the same thing at the same time. The reader-person becomes a reader-personage. This dimension shifts back and forth as we turn from the *Morelliana* chapters to those of "Del lado de acá" and "Del lado de allá."

There is, in fact, a whole series of dimensional shifts in *Rayuela*. It is almost as if the novel consisted of a network of different dimensions, constantly changing, never static. For example, not only are Oliveira and the Club members accomplice-readers, but also Morelli. A frequent situation in the "De otros lados" chapters is that of Morelli quoting and/or commenting on a given text (e.g., Chapters 62 and 86). This is a case of the interaction of three roles: personage, novelist, reader. It would even be reasonable to assume that Morelli's writing contributed significantly to Oliveira's life, ". . . a mutarlo, a desplazarlo, a enajenarlo" (497–98).

This is extremely interesting for the inner dynamics of the novel. But if we take seriously Morelli-Cortázar's ideas about the reader's role, we must realize that they also point toward an outer, extra-literary direction – toward us, the readers. Herein lies the disappointing element to which I referred above. First of all, Cortázar's terminology regarding the reader is unnecessary and even obscurantist. What is the *lector-cómplice*, for example, if not an intelligent reader whose sensibilities permit him to penetrate superficial levels of meaning? Secondly, the whole idea of the *lector-cómplice* suggests that the barriers dividing life and literature be destroyed or, at least, removed. If this situation were fully realized, would not the novelist's responsibility for his own creation be reduced considerably? This shared responsibility would indeed make the role of the reader more active but could also make that of the novelist more passive.

For the most part, Cortázar's novel exemplifies Morelli's theories. Both Cortázar and Morelli are *voyants* as novelists, rather than *voyeurs*, in that they both take active roles in their writings, that is, they write about the problems of writing. Regarding descriptive techniques, we cannot say that Cortázar has done away with them entirely, as Morelli would have it. One of the strongest scenes in *Rayuela* is the Berthe Trépat episode, constructed with highly descriptive techniques. The extrapolation idea in which the personages jump toward us or we toward them finds expression when Oliveira and the Club members read Morelli along with us. The idea of the comic novel and the anthropophany is certainly put into practice, especially in the Buenos Aires section of the novel. Needless to say, Cortázar coins the word anthropophany to refer to the revelation or manifestation of authentic, human values. What can be more anthropophanous than the mutual concern and friendship between Oliveira and Traveler (especially as displayed in Chapter 56)? Also practised by Cortázar are Morelli's ideas about the anti-novel. *Rayuela* is, without a doubt, "un texto desaliñado, desanudado, incongruente . . ." (452) which possesses, at the same time, a certain plot outline, skeletal and sketchy though it may be, and occasional traditionally wrought passages (Berthe Trépat). This last element would correspond to the Morellian edict: ". . . sin vedarse los grandes efectos del género cuando la situación lo requiera . . ." (452). The anti-novel that Morelli proposes as a catalyst of confused notions (the wooden board scene) and as a vehicle which gives rise to openings and other dimensions (the role of the reader) is also most definitely realized by Cortázar.

In a broader sense, the ideas about literature in general expressed by Morelli can also be said to be characteristic of *Rayuela* as a whole. The main idea here is the concept of anti-literature, an amplified view of the anti-novel. As we have seen, Morelli characterizes his anti-literature as being essentially the practice of taking-away-from. In this respect, the taking away of completely logical categories, such as those found in psychological literature, definitely applies to *Rayuela*. As we have already seen, logical categories are not completely destroyed in *Rayuela*, but this situation does not contradict Morelli. It fits into his concept of anti-literature as only a partial rejection, ". . . puesto que se apoya en la palabra" (452). In conclusion, even considering this attitude of compromise in Morelli, we can still see how he is more revolutionary than his creator. Morelli says that nothing can be denounced as long as it is done within the same system as the object of denunciation (509). *Rayuela* itself serves as eloquent testimony against that point of view. In *Rayuela* Cortázar has denounced the custom and habit of literature without completely rejecting the "system," that is, traditional means of expression.

The quest I have attempted to illuminate in this chapter is a parallel one, undertaken by Oliveira on the vital level and by Morelli on the literary. This dual quest should be judged a failure, not because of its inherent negativism (the rejection of traditional, formulaic order), but rather because of more concrete considerations. In the case of Oliveira, his quest ends in insanity. With regard to Morelli, his quest remains provocative, but only on the theoretical level. *Rayuela* does not present the reader with Morelli's fiction but rather with that of Cortázar. And in the peculiar structuring of his novel, in his extraordinary consciousness of language and forceful stylistic expression, Julio Cortázar is successful. I shall try to indicate the nature of this success in the following chapters.

2 *Structures*

The initiated reader, once aware of the paradoxical nature of *Rayuela*, begins to realize the true direction of this novel. The destruction which Morelli proposes and which Cortázar carries out (only to a certain extent, as indicated in my previous chapter) is no more than a means to a constructive end – an authentic literature, an authentic reality. What carries apparently negative force results in essentially positive effects. With this in mind, it should be no surprise that the seemingly formless mass of *Rayuela* is not at all formless, but rather contains certain structural patterns and features which directly relate to Cortázar's vision (see *4*).

An analysis of the external structure of the novel reveals a method of composition based on groupings of two. The first such grouping is encountered at the outset. Cortázar indicates that *Rayuela* is composed mainly of two books, one that is read in the customary manner through Chapter 56, the remaining 99 chapters being "expendable," and the other by skipping back and forth according to the indications supplied, a method which encompasses all 155 chapters.[7] This dual scheme also has parallels within the novel itself, as in the case of Chapter 55, for example. In the second book referred to by Cortázar, there is no numerical indication for Chapter 55. On first glance, it seems to have disappeared. In an interesting article, Juan Loveluck suggests that one result of reading *Rayuela* the second way is "no llegar a un

[7] It is interesting to note that in editions subsequent to the first (1963), Cortázar adds a sentence to the "Tablero de dirección." In the first edition we read, "A su manera este libro es muchos libros, pero sobre todo es dos libros," after which follow the instructions for the two ways of reading. In the second and subsequent editions, one observes the additional : "El lector queda invitado *a elegir* una de las dos posibilidades siguientes." It is obvious that Cortázar added this comment in response to critical appraisal of *Rayuela* and for the purpose of clarifying, if not his intentions, at least his motives. It was thought that the two books suggested by Cortázar and the respectively different manners of reading them was a mere guise to fool the reader into reading Chapters 1–56 for a second time. By adding the new sentence, Cortázar implies that no such trick was intended, and that he was sincere in suggesting two books or two different ways of reading his book.

capítulo que en este orden de lectura desaparece, se fantasmiza:
el 55" (*8*, p. 85). The fact is, however, that Chapter 55 does
reappear verbatim in the "second" book, but in a rather disguised
form. Chapter 55 becomes part of Chapters 129 and 133, where
Cortázar introduces the reader to Ceferino Piriz's absurd plan for
world peace entitled "La Luz de la Paz del Mundo." Another
more apparent parallel to the dual structure of the novel is its
physical setting: Paris and Buenos Aires.

Doubles

Apart from the purely external considerations, one continues to
find dual structures. The most obvious manifestation of this
tendency is seen in *Rayuela*'s personages. I have already mentioned the identification of Oliveira and Morelli with their
creator. They are doubles of Cortázar. Perhaps a more
accurate term would be halves, since Oliveira expresses Cortázar's
metaphysical preoccupations and Morelli the literary. I do not
mean to suggest that they are mere symbols without human significance. It is true that the reader knows much more about Oliveira
than about Morelli, but the latter is, nevertheless, a personage of
the novel who is living out the rest of his life in a hospital in
Paris. And even though they both represent different aspects of
the same man, as personages Oliveira and Morelli maintain a
certain amount of autonomy.[8] The fact remains, however, that
they are two likenesses which reflect Cortázar's attempt to
identify "el sentido de la condición humana con su sentido de la
condición de artista" (539).

The important element to note is that the concept of sets or
pairs of two (doubles, in the case of personages) forms a basic
structural component of *Rayuela*.[9] The most evident set of doubles

[8] See Chapter 99, especially pp. 504–05, where Oliveira seems to misunderstand
Morelli when the former insists: "Pero el mismo Morelli no ve más que el lado
negativo de su guerra. Siente que tiene que hacerla, como vos y como todos
nosotros. ¿Y?" Cortázar employs Etienne to explain that "la lección de Morelli
basta como primera etapa" and that what he really wants to do is "quebrar
los hábitos mentales del lector" because Morelli "busca una interacción menos
mecánica."

[9] See Marta Morello-Frosch, "El personaje y su doble en las ficciones de
Cortázar," *Revista Iberoamericana*, XXXIV, No. 66 (julio-diciembre 1968), 323–30.
Frosch studies this concept of the double in Cortázar's short stories, and shows
how it contributes "posibilidades de enriquecimiento vital" to his prose.

is Oliveira and Traveler. The reader will recall that Oliveira and Traveler are about the same age and are of similar background and physical appearance. Talita coments frequently on their similarity. They themselves recognize that one is the *Doppelgänger,* or second self, of the other, but Cortázar does not really make clear which self is the original and which the second. What is perfectly clear, though, is the fact that Traveler is what Oliveira would have been had he not left Buenos Aires. Whereas Oliveira, dissatisfied with his situation in Buenos Aires, had left for Paris,

> Traveler no le echaba la culpa a la vida o a la suerte por no haber podido viajar a gusto. Simplemente se bebía una ginebra de un trago, y se trataba a sí mismo de cretinacho. (257)

So the personage Traveler is a characterization based upon Oliveira's (and, we may assume, Cortázar's) past. In a sense, this past is brought up to date in the person of Traveler. He represents the projection of an imagined future (Oliveira's, had he remained in Argentina).

This is also the case with the other set of doubles in the novel, La Maga and Talita, but in a slightly different sense. There is no striking physical resemblance between the two women, as is the case with their male counterparts. The women are also different in the sense that La Maga was without formal education and culturally ignorant; Talita, on the other hand, is a graduate pharmacist who expresses interest in "pueblos nómades" and "culturas trashumantes" (257). Nevertheless, even with these differences, as far as Oliveira is concerned La Maga and Talita become as if they were one person. From the moment he steps off the boat on his return to Buenos Aires, he begins to identify Talita with La Maga. This identification grows ever more intense till it becomes almost absolute in Chapter 56. On the brink of utter insanity and suicide, Oliveira refers to Talita in his conversation with Traveler and calls her La Maga. The following dialog ensues:

> ¿Ahora es a propósito que le llamás la Maga? No mientas, Horacio.
> — Yo sé que es Talita, pero hace un rato era la Maga. Es las dos, como nosotros.
> — Eso se llama locura — dijo Traveler. (401)

The significant difference, then, between the two pairs of doubles – Oliveira and Traveler, La Maga and Talita – is that in the former case, the above-mentioned projection is recognized both by the personages and by the reader. Oliveira and Traveler are recognized as doubles by each other, by Talita, and by the reader. This is not the case with the female doubles. Oliveira alone identifies Talita with La Maga.

The doubling of La Maga and Talita is also a projection of an imagined future, but in a different and more restricted sense. When Oliveira left Paris, he did not know what had become of La Maga. She had returned to Montevideo or had gone to Italy or had thrown herself into the Seine or was still living somewhere in Paris. Only when Oliveira returns to Argentina and begins to imagine that he sees La Maga (the woman on the boat, for example) does he realize that he is in love with her: "Saberse enamorado de la Maga no era un fracaso ni una fijación en un orden caduco . . ." (338). When he first sees Talita, the force of his desire to see La Maga again brings about the La Maga-Talita identification. He had previously concluded, while inquiring about La Maga in Montevideo, that his search for her had meaning:

> . . . así la Maga dejaría de ser un objeto perdido para volverse la imagen de una posible reunión – pero no ya con ella sino más acá o más allá de ella; por ella, pero no ella –. (340)

This possibility is realized when he meets Talita and projects the image. Talita becomes La Maga as well as retaining her own identity. This constitutes the projection of imagination on a spatial level rather than a temporal one, as was the case with Traveler-Oliveira. The projection of the La Maga-Talita double is based not so much on Oliveira's past experience as on a contemporary experience but in a different place – Paris.[10]

[10] It could be argued that, once Oliveira is in Buenos Aires, his relationship with La Maga could literally be considered a past experience, thereby invalidating my temporal-spatial distinction between the male and female pairs of doubles. But considering that there is no spatial transference when Cortázar imagines Traveler as a double to Oliveira, and that La Maga is part of Oliveira's immediate, rather than remote, past, the distinction would hold true.

Opposites

This aspect of doubles is but one side of the coin, of the characteristic groupings of two in the novel. The other side of the coin also deals with sets of two, those which exhibit dissimilarities, however, rather than likenesses. These contrary concepts appear throughout and form an integral part of the novel. No classification is absolutely satisfactory, but since I referred above to doubles, it is fitting to refer to these paradoxes, contrasts, contradictions, and polarizations as opposites. I have already noted a striking example of this characteristic in my last chapter, the essentially positive foundation beneath Morelli's proposals to destroy the novel, to destroy literature. And in a more explicit way, the narrator comments on the basis of the difficulty with which Morelli writes:

> Ahora sólo podía escribir laboriosamente, examinando a cada paso *el posible contrario* [italics mine], la escondida falacia . . . , sospechando que toda idea clara era siempre error o verdad a medias, desconfiando de las palabras que tendían a organizarse eufónica, rítmicamente, con el ronroneo feliz que hipnotiza al lector después de haber hecho su primera víctima en el escritor mismo. (502)

Oliveira himself expresses similar thoughts, though on a more social level, at the beginning of the novel. Thinking about his youth and his pontificating relatives, whose authoritarian "¡Se lo digo yo!" characterized their language, he reflects on how he later discovered this form of egocentrism to be widespread.

> Más tarde le hizo gracia comprobar cómo en las formas superiores de cultura el peso de las autoridades y las influencias, la confianza que dan las buenas lecturas y la inteligencia, producían también su "se lo digo yo" finamente disimulado, incluso para el que lo profería: ahora se sucedían los "siempre he creído", "si de algo estoy seguro", "es evidente que", *casi nunca compensado por una apreciación desapasionada del punto de vista opuesto* [italics mine]. (33)

In summary, the concept of "opposites" – the "punto de vista opuesto," the "posible contrario" – is roundly expressed by both Morelli and Oliveira. A close analysis of the text yields a greater variety of references, all of which may be classified as pairs of opposites. The significance of the above quotations is that they indicate Cortázar's conscious preoccupation with this sort of structure.

The pairs of opposites occur within three main frames of reference in the novel: [11]

(1) characterization and interaction of personages
(2) sight and sound
(3) abstract notions dealing with truth and reality

Regarding the first category, Oliveira describes the life he and La Maga lead in Paris, saying that "El desorden en que vivíamos . . . me parecía una disciplina necesaria" (25). Along similar lines, Oliveira characterizes his past life as "una penosa estupidez porque se quedaba en mero movimiento dialéctico, en la elección de una inconducta en vez de una conducta . . ." (25). On the one hand, disorder as discipline and the selection of a non-conduct are not precisely opposites but rather parallel elements of a phrase which have basically conflicting connotations. It is not usual to associate discipline with disorder, behavioral choice with non-conduct (one seems to cancel out the other). On the other hand, these conflicting pairs stand out precisely because Cortázar has chosen to associate concepts that are the very opposite of those expected, anticipated by the reader. And he puts these contrasts and opposites into a context which makes the opposition not only reasonable and understandable but also necessary. The structural opposition of concepts in the above examples seems necessary to illustrate best one of the significant themes of *Rayuela*. In both examples, it is clear that Oliveira is referring to the positive act of escaping the mould, petrification, habit.

Other instances of Oliveira's self-characterization reveal a more direct pair of opposites. At one point, Oliveira reflects on his ten-

[11] I use these three categories as a convenient scheme which will best permit me to illustrate the presence of opposites in the novel. I do not mean to suggest any notion of fixed categories. That is to say, it is conceivable that the reader may be able to find even more than the three basic groups I mention. Also, references to opposites in *Rayuela* occur on many levels – thematic, structural, stylistic – so I wish to point out that my rather arbitrary division is intended to be representative rather than exhaustive.

dency to be not a man of action but an active spectator, incapable of action without previous reflection. Summing up this characteristic, Oliveira thinks: "Mi fuerza está en mi debilidad" (476).

At times Oliveira will allude to the concept of opposites in his self-characterization merely by using one word in place of the expected one. For example, when La Maga first tells Oliveira that it would be best if he were to leave her, he responds:

– Probablemente. Fijate, de todas maneras, que si me voy ahora cometo algo que se parece casi al heroísmo, es decir que te dejo sola, sin plata y con tu hijo enfermo. (103)

The pair of opposites here is encompassed in the word heroism. Why would his leaving her be almost as if it were an heroic act? Evidently, the projected act would be one of such extreme cowardice that it would resemble the opposite value – heroism. This particular example of opposites differs from the above-mentioned in that a noun (heroism) is contrasted with an entire act (the prospect of his leaving) rather than with another expressed noun (disorder/discipline).

Aside from characterization, a glance at the interaction of characters also reveals a structuring based on opposites. Perhaps the most patent example of this is seen in the relationship and interaction of Horacio and La Maga. He is troubled by his inability to shake off his all-pervasive intellectuality, and he stands as an opposite to La Maga who, with her spontaneous, intuitive nature, tries half-heartedly to educate herself. I have already discussed this aspect of their relationship and its significance as theme in the previous chapter. This relationship also merits consideration for what it reveals about structure, about opposites. Very early in the novel Horacio declares: ". . . yo me sentía antagónicamente cerca de la Maga, nos queríamos en una dialéctica de imán y limadura, de ataque y defensa, de pelota y pared" (26). And her relationship with the other Club members was on the same level. Soon after her disappearance, Etienne says: "La pobre entendía tan bien muchas cosas que ignorábamos a fuerza de saberlas" (606). This also expresses why the "ignorant" La Maga is able to give the "cultured" Horacio "lecciones sobre la manera de mirar y de ver" (37). This apparent contradiction, the pecu-

liar situation of La Maga vis-à-vis the other characters in the
novel, could be classified as mere paradox were it not for the role
it has as part of a recurrent ordering or pattern throughout the
novel; this pattern consists of a separation into two contrasting
units which I have called opposites. On the one hand, this very
quality of opposites is what prevents the normal development of
the love relationship between Horacio and La Maga. By normal
I mean not bestial and primitivistic, as depicted in the sexual en-
counter in Chapter 5. There the reader is told that Horacio and
La Maga "casi nunca se alcanzaban porque en pleno diálogo
eran tan distintos y andaban por tan opuestas cosas . . ."(45). On
the other hand, this contrastive nature of their relationship is its
very foundation and strength.

The pattern of opposites extends its frequent references to the
auditory and visual senses. Cortázar's concept of silence is interesting. It may be the "silencio ensordecedor" which Oliveira
used to experience whenever he saw a woman who resembled
La Maga (15). This is an active silence, a silence with the capacity
to deafen, a characteristic usually attributed to loud noise, that is,
the opposite of silence. But silence may have other "opposite"
concepts, music for instance. How can the polarity of silence on
the one hand and music on the other possibly express any experience other than one of difference? In order to answer this question, it will be necessary to examine three significant references in
Rayuela to the relationship between silence and music.

First, there is the moment when Horacio reflects on the love
relationship, essentially unsatisfactory, between him and La
Maga.

> Tan triste oyendo al cínico Horacio que quiere un amor pasa-
> porte, amor pasamontañas, amor llave, amor revólver, amor
> que le dé los mil ojos de Argos, la ubicuidad, *el silencio desde
> donde la música es posible* [italics mine], la raíz desde donde
> se podría empezar a tejer una lengua. (483)

In the italicized clause above, Cortázar reduces the polarities of
the silence-music relationship. Here the concept of silence is seen
as a prerequiste in order that a musical experience may follow.
And just as there must be a previous silence in order for music to

be possible, so must there be a certain "root" state, a certain
purification of, in, and through literature in order that a genuine
language may begin to be woven. We have already seen how
Morelli and Cortázar strive toward that end.

Cortázar uses a similar image during one of the jazz sessions
of the Club. After one of the records had ended,

> . . . la crepitación de la púa mientras el disco seguía girando y
> el silencio que había en toda música verdadera se desarrimaba
> lentamente de las paredes, salía de debajo del diván, se despe-
> gaba como labios o capullos. (68)

But here the author refers to silence as a continuum, displaced
while the music was playing, only to return after the music had
ended. Cortázar seems to speak of silence here as being *in* music
in the sense that the quality of the music played will determine
the intensity of the silence that follows. The better the music, the
more intense the silence. In any case, this exemplifies another way
in which Cortázar has reduced the polarization. He uses two
inherently different categories – silence and sound (music) – in
a way which associates and almost unites the two concepts in a
single category.

In a reference to sound and silence later in the novel, both of
the above interrelationships combine to enrich the metaphor used
by the author. Commenting on the ambiguity of Morelli's work,
the narrator writes of the fascinated consternation of the Club
members. We read:

> Si algún consuelo les quedaba era pensar que también Morelli
> se movía en esa misma ambigüedad, orquestando una obra
> cuya legítima primera audición debía ser quizá el más absoluto
> de los silencios. (604-05)

Here again are two linguistic elements, two nouns which, in a
denotative sense, express extreme difference (almost opposition) –
"audición" and "silencios." But instead of using them in this
contrastive, customary manner, Cortázar employs them in an
associative, complementary sense. The first hearing of Morelli's
literary work clearly refers to the first stage of his goals – the
destructive part, the anti-literature, the un-writing – in effect,
what the Morelliana chapters express and what portions of

Cortázar's narrative exemplify. As we have already seen, this is mainly a purifying process, breaking the habit of logically ordered literary categories in the search for authentic expression. Once accomplished, once heard (continuing the above metaphor), there would then exist "the silence whence music is possible," the silence as prerequisite. Cortázar's metaphor also demands the other level of meaning – silence as continuum. The excellence of Morelli's "legítima primera audición," then, determines "quizá el más absoluto de los silencios," which may well refer to the difficulty in understanding a literature such as that proposed by Morelli.

What is important to observe, however, is the noticeable structure, the pairs of opposites that Cortázar employs in both explicit and subtle manners in his novel. In addition to the auditory sense, the visual sense is also explored by the author and the opposites are extracted. In Chapter 1, Oliveira mentions a section of Paris where the Club members used to meet "para hablar con un vidente ciego, paradoja estimulante" (19). The tone of this reference to the "blind seer" here seems to be playful and without further transcendence. But Oliveira mentions how stimulating the paradox is. The reader is not surprised, then, that Oliveira uses an almost identical paradox in Chapter 98, when he begins to realize the true worth of La Maga. The chapter begins with the following statements:

Y así es cómo los que nos iluminan son los ciegos. Así es cómo alguien, sin saberlo, llega a mostrarte irrefutablemente un camino que por su parte sería incapaz de seguir. (499)

The two examples above, though not especially daring in their execution, serve to show that Cortázar's tendency to reduce or approximate opposites remains a constant feature of the novel. This image of the blind seer, the blind who illuminate, is used in a rather impersonal, almost aphoristic manner in the above examples. Oliveira also uses a very similar image in a more personal way, referring to himself. In effect, this amounts to Oliveira's having to close his eyes in order to see better. First, with regard to La Maga, Oliveira relates that upon first meeting her, he realized that in order to enter into her world, ". . . para verte como yo quería era necesario empezar por cerrar los ojos. . ." (18). Then, when first back in Buenos Aires, he finds himself not doing much of anything except sleeping and glancing at a book he had discovered at the bottom of his suitcase. He explains his lethargy:

> De esa fiaca tan metódica no podía resultar nada bueno, y él confiaba vagamente en eso, en que entrecerrando los ojos se vieran algunas cosas mejor dibujadas, de que durmiendo se le aclararan las meninges. (271)

We should recall that "esa fiaca tan metódica" is a phrase borrowed from Traveler, who used it to characterize Oliveira's avoidance of political and occupational pursuits. In both examples, Oliveira seems to feel that he can obtain a more acute sense of a given reality (La Maga's world, the whole Buenos Aires experience) by first closing his eyes to it (literally, in the La Maga example) or by at least blurring his vision ("entrecerrando los ojos").

The same kinds of polarization occur on all levels. In the realm of abstract concepts, for example, there exists throughout the novel a constant true/false displacement. At the beginning of the novel, Oliveira tells of the moment when La Maga first began to tell him about her rather sordid past. Oliveira reacts: "Cómo podía yo sospechar que aquello que parecía tan mentira era verdadero . . ." (18). Then later, while observing La Maga as she is about to utter "alguna de sus burradas," Oliveira "Sintió una especie de ternura rencorosa, algo tan contradictorio que debía ser la verdad misma" (52). In the chapter dealing with the death of Rocamadour, Oliveira tries to verbalize his personal concept of absurdity, but Etienne complains that it lacks clarity. Oliveira replies: "No puede estar claro, si lo estuviera sería falso, sería científicamente verdadero quizá, pero falso como absoluto" (195). In the first instance, what appears to be a lie turns out to be true. Then Oliveira identifies an inner feeling that is so contradictory that it must be truth itself. Finally, we see that a concept expressed with the greatest clarity may be scientifically true but still be basically false. In fact, the whole process of explanation, the attempt to shed light and truth in a rational, logical manner is, we are told, "un error bien vestido" (329).

Triads

This dual aspect is not the only structural arrangement to be
emphasized in *Rayuela*. There also exists a pattern of triads or
groupings of three.[12] Needless to say, the external design that
introduces this characteristic is seen in the division of the novel
into the sections "Del lado de allá," "Del lado de acá," and "De
otros lados (*Capítulos prescindibles*)". But this division into
triads also extends into more internal aspects of the novel. It is
not a mere mechanical device such as that used by Carlos Fuentes
in *La muerte de Artemio Cruz*.

Upon examining the personages, the human groups in the
novel, the reader notices the same tendency to tripartite composition. In Paris, Horacio and La Maga become part of a "love
triangle" when Gregorovius enters the scene and becomes interested in La Maga. The reader is reminded of this grouping into
three whenever Horacio expresses his jealousy to La Maga or to
Gregorovius – a frequent occurrence. Thus, the triad exists not
only when the three personages are physically present in a given
situation in the novel. The figure of the triad or triangle, the
tripartite situation, is strengthened and focussed whenever the
reader encounters a human emotion resulting from the situation.
This emotion usually consists of Oliveira's suspicion and accu-

[12] I am not the only one to have noticed this tripartite arrangement, but to
the best of my knowledge, it has not been examined closely. Juan Loveluck
points out two sets of triads in the novel (*8*, pp. 86–87). One consists of the
formal division of the book into three parts and the other results from what
Loveluck calls "el juego de tres capas geológicamente ordenadas." First, there
is a "cuerpo fictivo," followed by two theoretical strata or levels which act as
a key to the former: "La que explica cierta clase de lectores o *antilectores* y
la que presenta una nueva teoría de la novela o *antinovela* en sí." The triad,
then, would consist of: 1) the fictive body, 2) the theory of the reader, and 3)
theory of the novel. Another mode of threeness – present in Cortázar's stories –
is suggested by Alfred J. MacAdam, *El individuo y el otro: crítica a los cuentos
de Julio Cortázar* (New York: La Librería, 1971). Also, cf. René Girard,
"Triangular Desire," in *Deceit, Desire, and the Novel: Self and Other in
Literary Structure*, trans. Yvonne Freccero (Baltimore: Johns Hopkins University
Press, 1965), pp. 1–52. For Girard, triangular desire is that which is formed by
a subject's imitation of a model (mediator) in order to reach his desired object.
Don Quijote imitates Amadís in order to realize the chivalric life, for example.
Girard uses his triangular arrangement of desire (subject-mediator-object) as a
critical means of approach to the novels of Cervantes, Flaubert, Stendhal,
Dostoyevsky, and Proust.

satory comments directed at both La Maga and Gregorovius (e.g., p. 97). A similar situation may be seen when Pola appears to form the third element of the figure. The figure of the triangle or triad stands out in this case when La Maga senses Pola's presence, a presence which seems to cling to Horacio. La Maga tells Ossip: "Pola es muy hermosa, lo sé por los ojos con que me miraba Horacio cuando volvía de estar con ella . . ." (164). And the triangle formed by Horacio, Talita, and Traveler in Buenos Aires presents the unusual structural circumstance of a triad of human triangles. These groupings of three, aside from their common characteristic as love triangles, have additional bonds of unity among them. First, Horacio figures in each of the triangles. Secondly, the common human emotion which emerges as a result of these triangles – jealousy – offers the reader further insight into the characters who display it. And just as we witnessed Cortázar's tendency to unite, reconcile, and bind concepts in the above discussion of opposites, so do we observe a like tendency in the case of the human triangles. In each of the three triangles mentioned, there is a different experience of jealousy by three different characters: Oliveira, La Maga, and Traveler. The ultimate result of this situation is that a new human triad is formed – Oliveira, La Maga and Traveler – by virtue of the common bond (the experience of jealousy) which unites them. This seems to be an example of what Cortázar means when he refers to the secret, hidden correspondences among certain people and things (see 2, pp. 227 ff.).

What is certain, though, is that Cortázar is conscious of this threeness of the human groups he creates. There are explicit references in the novel to support this belief. After La Maga's disappearance, it is suggested to Oliveira that she had moved in with Pola, acting as a nurse. Before deciding not to verify this clue to La Maga's whereabouts, Oliveira reflects:

– Yo en realidad tendría que ir – le dijo Oliveira a un gato negro de la rue Danton –. Una cierta obligación estética, completar la figura. El tres, la Cifra. (238)

Most of the explicit references, however, deal with the Oliveira/ Talita/Traveler triad. Regarding the relationship among these three personages, the reader is told: "Por debajo de los temas de discusión circulaba siempre un aire patafísico, la triple coincidencia en una histriónica búsqueda de puntos de mira que excentraran al mirador o a lo mirado" (269). In this case, Alfred Jarry's word "pataphysical"[13] is used to characterize the other reality sensed from the "triple coincidencia" of the personages. Then there is the incident of the wooden board, after which Talita recognizes herself as the fulcrum between two scales – in effect, another triad (311). Finally, there is the instance when Oliveira realizes the disconcerting effect he has on the relationship between Talita and Traveler. In a conversation with Traveler in which he offers to leave them in peace, as they were before his arrival from Paris, Oliveira mentions Talita and the following exchange occurs:

– A Talita dejala afuera.
– No – dijo Oliveira –. Ni pienso dejarla afuera. Nosotros somos Talita, vos y yo, un triángulo sumamente trismegístico. (328-29)

Here again he refers to the figure of the triangle and qualifies it with the adjective trismegistic, referring to the mysterious, hermetic nature of the relationship between the three personages. This kind of relationship is brought about, as we have already seen, by the doubling of different personages through time-space fusions and associations.

There are also individual scenes in the novel that suggest a preoccupation with threeness. In the Berthe Trépat concert, for example (Chapter 23), there is an extraordinary threeness to the whole episode. There are three musical compositions on the program, each one of which exhibits different tripartite character-

---

[13] See Martin Esslin, *The Theatre of the Absurd* (Garden City, N.Y.: Doubleday, 1965), pp. 258–59. Here Esslin speaks of pataphysics as being originally a burlesque on science. See also "Exploits and Opinions of Doctor Faustroll, Pataphysician: A Neo-Scientific Novel," trans. Simon Watson Taylor, in *Selected Works of Alfred Jarry*, ed. Roger Shattuck and Simon Watson Taylor (New York: Grove Press, 1965), p. 192, where Jarry himself explains pataphysics as the science of the particular and the exceptional that describes a world which can and should be envisaged in place of the traditional one. On the basis of this concept alone, it is not difficult to understand Cortázar's appreciation for the alleged grandfather of Surrealism.

istics. The first contains three movements ("Tres movimientos discontinuos"). The second piece, "Pavana para el General Leclerc," has three themes (129). In the third piece, the "Síntesis Délibes—Saint–Saëns," the threeness is realized through the collaborative efforts of the music's three distinguished composers – Délibes, Saint-Saëns, and the inimitable Berthe Trépat.

By far the most interesting chapter in *Rayuela,* for what it suggests regarding the novel's two and three-fold arrangement, is Chapter 139. Before examining this chapter, let us consider for a moment the entire section, "De otros lados (*Capítulos prescindibles*)." In James Irby's review of *Hopscotch,*[14] he pays tribute to the importance of the Morelliana chapters of this section, but he also accurately summarizes the general characteristics of all these expendable characters with the following description:

> Many of the additional chapters are only a few lines in length. Some explain certain gaps and allusions in the main narrative (mostly in Paris), leaving others to be surmised. Some are quotations from books or newspapers which may serve as glosses or sources as one sees fit. Some are further notes and meditations by Oliveira.

This is certainly so. However, it seems that these comments stress the participatory role of this part of the novel insofar as it may shed light upon another part (either a specific incident, chapter, or group of chapters). I should like to suggest a possibility more comprehensive in scope. Indeed, these chapters act as "glosses or sources," but some refer or allude to the novel in its entirety. Certainly many of the *Morelliana* chapters serve in this capacity, almost as if they were keys to unlock some of the mysteries of the narrative. And with respect to the subject under discussion, Chapter 139 exemplifies just such a key to the novel's structural composition. This chapter is situated toward the end of the novel and consists of a one-page anonymous commentary taken by Cortázar from a recording of an Alban Berg Chamber Concerto. The anonymous commentator begins by pointing out the musical anagram of the piece; certain notes of the piano, violin, and

[14] "Cortázar's *Hopscotch* and Other Games," *Novel: A Forum on Fiction,* No. 1 (Fall 1967), p. 65.

horn represent the names of the composers Schoenberg, Webern, and Berg himself. Then the chapter comes to an end with the following remarks:

> Otra analogía significativa con el futuro Concierto para violín consiste en la estricta simetría del conjunto. En el Concierto para violín el número clave es dos: dos movimientos separados, dividido cada uno de ellos en dos partes, además de la división violín-orquesta en el conjunto instrumental. En el "Kammer-konzert" se destaca, en cambio, el número tres: la dedicatoria representa al Maestro y a sus dos discípulos; los instrumentos están agrupados en tres categorías: piano, violín y una com-binación de instrumentos de viento; su arquitectura es una con-strucción en tres movimientos encadenados, cada uno de los cuales revela en mayor o menor medida una composición tri-partita. (599)

What I suggest, then, on the basis of the ubiquitous patterns of twos and threes I have indicated above, is that this Chapter 139 reflects this arrangement as it exists throughout the whole novel.

What does this all mean? Are these twos and threes merely aesthetic decoration? I think not. In the course of a review of *Hopscotch* (*New York Review of Books,* April 28, 1966, pp. 17-19), John Wain states that the novel's essence has to do with the exploration of new modes of consciousness. This is true. But to say that Cortázar attempts to change the consciousness of the reader by expanding it requires some explanation. Chapter 116 is interesting for what it reveals about the concept of con-sciousness. Morelli cites the art critic Lionello Venturi on the singularity of Manet. Venturi said that at a time when the repre-sentation of reality was becoming more and more objective, that is, photographic and mechanical, Manet in his quest for realism came to understand art as a series of images, a tendency practiced in medieval art. His concentration on the plastic image, then, implied a return of modern art to the Middle Ages. Manet's con-tribution was to "devolver el arte a su función de creador de imágenes . . ." (545). Morelli-Cortázar then proceeds to outline his concept of *figura*:[15]

[15] For a thorough treatment of both the etymology of the word *figura* and the historical development of figural interpretation from antiquity through the

Acostumbrarse a emplear la expresión *figura* en vez de *imagen*, para evitar confusiones. Sí, todo coincide. Pero no se trata de una vuelta a la Edad Media ni cosa parecida. Error de postular un tiempo histórico absoluto: Hay tiempos diferentes *aunque* paralelos. En ese sentido, uno de los tiempos de la llamada Edad Media puede coincidir con uno de los tiempos de la llamada Edad Moderna. Y ese tiempo es el percibido y habitado por pintores y escritores que rehúsan apoyarse en la circunstancia, ser 'modernos' en el sentido en que lo entienden los contemporáneos, lo que no significa que opten por ser anacrónicos; sencillamente están al margen del tiempo superficial de su época, y desde ese otro tiempo donde todo accede a la condición de *figura,* donde todo vale como signo y no como tema de descripción, intentan una obra que puede parecer ajena o antagónica a su tiempo y a su historia circundantes, y que sin embargo los incluye, los explica, y en último término los orienta hacia una trascendencia en cuyo término está esperando el hombre. (545)

This passage serves as an excellent starting point in our discussion of the expansion of consciousness. We see here a denial of linear, chronological time. Morelli proposes a parallelism of different times that may be perceived by those artists and writers who are capable of seeing beyond the superficial (e.g., historical time), those who can see the *figura* to be formed by the fusion of analogous concepts, persons, and acts existing in historically different temporal categories (Middle Ages, Modern Age).

This is precisely what the dynamics of the novel reveal through its patterns of twos and threes. The structures of both the doubles and the opposites adhere to this same concept. Certain characters (Oliveira/Morelli, Oliveira/Traveler, and La Maga/Talita) were doubles in spite of their differences (metaphysical/literary and time/space differences). In the case of opposites, we have already seen how Cortázar tends to reconcile them, unite them, show their interdependency and dissolve them. In short, he shows the

Middle Ages, see Erich Auerbach's essay "Figura," trans. Ralph Manheim, in *Scenes from the Drama of European Literature* (New York: Meridian Books, 1959), pp. 11–76. For a discussion of the figural concept in Cortázar's *Los premios*, see *10* pp. 99–109.

oneness of opposites.[16] It is not by mere chance that the name Heraclitus appears with such frequency throughout the novel,[17] especially at the end of the first section.

The triple patterns contribute a certain cyclic rhythm to the novel. In the light of the temporal fusions referred to above, the triad structures would seem to reflect the basic time divisions of past, present, and future. But the groupings of three also allude to a more transcendental concept. It is clear throughout the novel that Cortázar feels that we must recover the hidden dimensions of our nature, of reality itself (cf. *10*, pp. 11-20). It is also clear that he considers the dualistic tradition of Western civilization to be a barrier to this achievement. A monistic consciousness is certainly not the answer, nor is dualism. Rather, a third way is called for, which may be perceived with the aid of an expanded consciousness. In Cortázar's own words:

> Puede ser que algún día quebremos y modifiquemos las circun-
> stancias del tiempo y del espacio y que nazca un nuevo hombre
> con ese tercer ojo, esa tercera mano de que hablan los tibetanos
> y a que yo aludo a veces en mis libros. (*7*, p. 13)

Rather than a logical, binary form of reasoning, Cortázar suggests an "analogous consciousness,"[18] consciousness of the *figura* to be formed by the unity of like structures which logical thought consigns to different categories. Not *YES* or *NO*, not *YES* and *NO*, but rather *YESNO*. This *YESNO* is a *figura* which repre-

---

[16] In a book which originally appeared in the same year as *Rayuela*, Alan W. Watts, *The Two Hands of God: The Myths of Polarity* (Toronto: Macmillan, 1969), presents the thesis of "man's perennial intuition of the implicit concord and harmony which underlies the explicit discord and conflict of life as he finds it with the naked eye, at the 'normal' level of magnification" (p. 41). Watts traces the oneness of opposites from Eastern myths and images, in which the inner unity of opposites is explicitly recognized; he shows how this unity disappears in Christian mythology with its notions of the complete separation between good and evil. Cortázar's interest in Eastern literature and culture is undeniable. Many of the dichotomies treated by Watts help clarify general notions of the unity of opposites as treated in *Rayuela*.

[17] Heraclitus considered fire to be the fundamental substance (cf. the "first" chapter of *Rayuela*, Chapter 73) and saw the unity of the world to be formed by the combination of opposites.

[18] See the entire passage by Pauwels and Bergier cited by Cortázar on pp. 466–67 of *Rayuela*, where a plea is made for "una conciencia analógica que asumiera las formas y asimilara los ritmos inconcebibles de esas estructuras profundas. . . ."

sents the harmony or unity of conflicting categories. There is nothing logical about it, but it is exceedingly human. The cipher three and its various patterns in *Rayuela* allude to this harmony, this third way, this expanded consciousness. It would be possible to point out the "openness" of *Rayuela* in many ways,[19] but this opening of consciousness sought by Cortázar is probably the most profound.

[19] For the most comprehensive study of openness of form as a common characteristic of contemporary culture, see Umberto Eco, *Opera aperta: forma e indeterminazione nelle poetiche contemporanee* (Milano: Bompiani, 1962). On literary openness there are at least two relatively recent books: Robert M. Adams, *Strains of Discord: Studies in Literary Openness* (Ithaca, N.Y.: Cornell University Press, 1958); Alan Friedman, *The Turn of the Novel* (New York: Oxford University Press, 1966). While Adams deals with openness as unresolved meaning in texts and authors ranging from Greek tragedies to Cervantes to Kafka, Friedman studies the openness of ethical experience in early twentieth-century English fiction. Even more pertinent to the subject under discussion, however, is Luis Gregorich, "*Tres tristes tigres*, obra abierta," *Nueva novela latinoamericana* I, ed. Jorge Lafforgue (Buenos Aires: Editorial Paidós, 1969), pp. 241–61. Gregorich uses Eco's study as a foundation from which to evaluate Guillermo Cabrera Infante's novel as representative of the entrance of the poetics of openness into the Hispanic novel. *Rayuela* is given perfunctory consideration and then is abruptly dismissed by Gregorich as "un esfuerzo convergente aunque no tan lúcido ni extremo, y cuyos artificios retóricos todavía deben demasiado al pasado" (p. 252).

3 Language and authenticity

Consciousness of Language

It is certainly apparent that Cortázar is concerned with language, but this concern is not remarkable in itself. Consciousness of language, furthermore, it is not merely a part of *Rayuela,* rather it is its very essence. Cortázar manifests an intense, all-pervading consciousness of language throughout the novel. On the one hand, Oliveira roams Paris seeking La Maga, seeking authenticity, seeking meaning in life, seeking a center, seeking the Heaven of the Hopscotch chart. On the other hand, he concerns himself, as in Chapter 3, with seemingly trivial problems of language while in a state of insomnia :

> Por la mañana tendría que ir a lo del viejo Trouille y ponerle al día la correspondencia con Latinoamérica. Salir, hacer, poner al día, no eran cosas que ayudaran a dormirse. Poner al día, vaya expresión. (31)

Here, at the beginning of the novel, Oliveira wonders over the most innocuous idiom, "poner al día." "Vaya expresión" seems to indicate Oliveira's consideration of a traditional or customary idiom as unusual or strange — at least strange enough to single out. This example is perfectly in accord with a characteristic of the novel which I pointed out in Chapter 1, namely the need to examine custom and habit for the sake of avoiding petrification and achieving an authentic literature. But language is the foundation of literature and this is where the examination must begin, not in any professional, scientific manner but rather by means of a novelist's having his protagonist halt in the midst of an insomniac rambling to question the legitimacy (the authenticity) of a taken-for-granted idiom.

The above example is not an isolated one. There are similar instances throughout the novel. When trying to describe a certain state of mind, Oliveira says :

> Es muy simple, toda exaltación o depresión me empuja a un
> estado propicio a
>> lo llamaré paravisiones
>> es decir (lo malo es eso, decirlo)
>> una aptitud instantánea para salirme. . . . (461)

In this case the parenthetical expression, though parallel to the
above "vaya expresión," contains an explicit affective quality.
Oliveira registers his annoyance with verbal expression as an in-
sufficient intermediary between subject (Oliveira) and object (his
paravisiones). But the similarity of this example to the one above
is clear. Both "poner al día" and "es decir," being frequently
used idioms, are commented upon, as if challenged, as if Cortázar
were saying: "These everyday expressions of the Spanish language which people have been using for who knows how long,
do they carry the same force they used to? Or are they clichés?
If they have become clichés, why not discard them?" The challenge offered by Cortázar in the above examples is somewhat
different in each case. "Vaya expresión" merely points toward
"poner al día" – as if the speaker were pausing to challenge
the authenticity of the expression without deciding upon a definite attitude to adopt. The parenthetical expression that chal-
lenges "es decir," on the other hand, is more definite since a
judgement is made, a definite attitude is expressed: "lo malo es
eso, decirlo."

Ineffectiveness of Language

This very same attitude toward language is developed to a fuller
degree when Oliveira continues to attempt to describe the state of
being of the above example. In the example below, notice that
first he attempts to describe, then criticizes the very desire to
do so:

> y en ese instante sé *lo que soy* porque estoy exactamente
> sabiendo *lo que no soy* (eso que ignoraré luego astutamente).
> Pero no hay palabras para una materia entre palabra y visión
> pura, como un bloque de evidencia. Imposible objetivar,
> precisar esa defectividad que aprehendí en el instante y que
> era *clara ausencia* o claro error o clara insuficiencia, pero
>> sin saber *de qué, qué*. (462)

The attitude expressed here documents the affective force of the above "es decir" example. Words do not suffice for Oliveira. He uses them to try to express what he feels, sees, thinks, but language is, in the end, ineffective as a means of expressing his vision of reality.

Proof of this ineffectiveness may be seen in the many ways in which Oliveira attempts to describe and define. Continuing with the above example we see that Oliveira, after realizing the insufficiency of language to express what he thinks and feels, frenetically seeks other means of description and definition. He tries to descibe, fails, then tries again, only to fail again:

> Otra manera de tratar de decirlo . . . Por ejemplo . . . Otra manera de querer decirlo . . . Es un poco así . . . es decir . . . .
> (462)

On the one hand, these phrases which introduce Oliveira's successive attempts to define and describe serve to underline his failure to do so. On the other hand, the expression of this failure is indeed positive and worthwhile.

This obsession with language in *Rayuela* occurs not only on the self-critical level. In an instance early in the novel, already cited in Chapter 1, La Maga criticizes Oliveira's language as being a reflection of his aloof manner of living. Oliveira had been speaking to her, half-admiringly and half-mockingly, of famous people who had chosen action-oriented ways of life. La Maga replies that Oliveira could never lead such a life because he thought too much before acting. The following exchange then ensues:

> — Parto del principio de que la reflexión debe preceder a la acción, bobalina.
> — Partís del principio — dijo La Maga —. Qué complicado. Vos sos como un testigo, sos el que va al museo y mira los cuadros. Quiero decir que los cuadros están ahí y vos en el museo, cerca y lejos al mismo tiempo. Yo soy un cuadro, Rocamadour es un cuadro. Etienne es un cuadro, esta pieza es un cuadro. Vos creés que estás en esta pieza pero no estás. Vos estás mirando la pieza, no estás en la pieza. (34)

La Maga here criticizes the cerebral, distant nature of Oliveira's language and consequently the reflective aloofness of his manner of living. The affective force of the criticism is one of disgust and pity at the same time. La Maga's repetition of "Partís del principio" also has the effect of an uncontrollable shudder caused by the icy blast of Oliveira's remark.

Mockery of Language

Cortázar's critical attitude toward language is not always expressed in a straightforward, serious manner. Sometimes the criticism is achieved with the use of mockery. At the end of the passage cited above, for example, La Maga was berating Oliveira for his inability to relate to people without examining them, for his inability to be ("Vos creés que estás en esta pieza pero no estás. Vos estás mirando la pieza, no estás en la pieza.") Oliveira, in turn, reacts by musing over La Maga's enviable character, so different from his own. Chapter 3 of the novel ends with his thinking:

> Feliz de ella que estaba dentro de la pieza, que tenía derecho de ciudad en todo lo que tocaba y convivía, pez río abajo, hoja en el arbol, nube en el cielo, imagen en el poema. Pez, hoja, nube, imagen: exactamente eso, a menos que . . . . (35)

In this chapter-ending Oliveira underscores the difference between him and La Maga by pointing out her uncomplicated view of the world in which fish swim downstream, leaves belong on trees, clouds in the sky and images in poems – an unchallenging acceptance of the natural orders of life and art. For contrast, recall Oliveira who cannot tolerate ". . . que el sol salga todos los días" (426). But the consciousness of language and the mockery involved in this passage are observed in the last sentence: "pez, hoja, nube, imagen: exactamente eso, a menos que . . .". Remember that Oliveira has just finished using the nouns in the first half of the sentence to indicate, by illustration, La Maga's uncomplicated, logically assimilated frame of reference vis-à-vis the world. The repetition and enumeration of the nouns, then, in this last sentence serve to sum up the image of La Maga which he had been forming in his mind. The next phrase, "exactamente eso," serves to reinforce and finalize the image just formed. For a split second Oliveira is satisfied in that language has been adequate to express, although in thought and not in speech, what has been his vision of reality (La Maga, in this case). But then the elliptical ending "a menos que . . ." suddenly criticizes and casts doubt upon the entire previous thought, his judgement of La Maga. Furthermore, the inchoate doubt registered by "a menos que" completely negates the validity of the phrase "exactamente eso" and, in effect, mocks the very existence of this phrase or any other similarly closed, absolute expression.

Cortázar mocks language in other ways. Frequently, in the midst of an intensely serious passage, he will revert to *hachismo* precisely to break the tension of the seriousness. Consider the example of Oliveira trying to describe the sensation of human limitation:

> Es un poco así: hay líneas de aire a los lados de tu cabeza, de tu mirada,
> zonas de detención de tus ojos, tu olfato, tu gusto,
> es decir que andás con tu límite *por fuera*
> y más allá de ese límite no podés llegar cuando creés que has aprehendido plenamente cualquier cosa, la cosa lo mismo que un iceberg tiene un pedacito por fuera y te lo muestra, y el resto enorme está más allá de tu límite y así es como se hundió el *Titanic*. Heste Holiveira siempre con sus hejemplos. (462-63)

On a general level, the addition of the "h" introduces a light, playful tone to counteract the weight of the serious language Oliveira had been using. The ultimate effect is anti-declamatory. On a more specific level, the *hachismo* here seems to poke fun at Oliveira's attempt to do precisely what he is pointing out to be impossible: to "apprehend something fully." This is exactly what Oliveira has been trying to do with language as his instrument of knowledge. He has been trying to pin down, to fully describe and define the sensation of human limitation. He is limited by the very language he uses and the *hachismo* of the final sentence seems at once to recognize this and mock the attempt. In both cases, the general and the specific, Cortázar mocks one kind of language by means of another kind. The serious is mocked by the playful; the language of description is mocked by the content of the passage, which indicates the impossibility of full description and definition. The *hachismo* in the latter instance underscores the paradox involved. Its affective force, after recognition of the paradox, is self-ridicule.

Another means Cortázar uses to mock his own seriousness is the frequent use of foreign words and expressions. Like the *hachismo,* these foreign words add a playful tone to the narrative.[20] Note the use of English and Italian in the example below where the narrator comments on the limits of imagination:

> Se ha elogiado en exceso la imaginación. La pobre no puede ir un centímetro más allá del límite de los seudópodos. Hacia acá, gran variedad y vivacidad. Pero en el otro espacio, donde sopla el viento cósmico que Rilke sentía pasar sobre su cabeza, Dame Imagination no corre. *Ho detto.* (464)

While it is certainly true that the entire tone of the passage is half-serious and half-frivolous, "Dame Imagination" and *"Ho detto"* emphasize the frivolity, the self-mockery.

Clichés

Cortázar's attitude toward the cliché is interesting in that rather than seeking to avoid its use in his novel, he utilizes it frequently precisely to ridicule it. For example, he will deride the hackneyed phrase or expression by stringing together the words which make up the phrase ("corriócomounreguerodepólvora" [492]) or by connecting them with a hyphen ("estaban-pendientes-de-sus-palabras" [349]). He singles out literary language and especially the literary cliché for criticism ranging from light derision to more severe, serious objection (see 6).[21] In a

[20] Some critics have indicated effects of a more serious nature in Cortázar's frequent use of foreign words and phrases, e.g. John G. Copeland, "Las imágenes de *Rayuela*", *Revista Iberoamericana*, XXXIII, No. 63 (enero-junio 1967), p. 93, writes: "Cierta palabra puede llegar a tener una fuerza más universal cuando se la traduce a varias lenguas, presentando así una serie de sinónimos que restauran a la palabra su vitalidad original." He then proceeds to outline and illustrate three specific effects of Cortázar's usage of foreign words: 1) as an aid in defining a given word, 2) as a way of adding a poetic dimension to the narrative, and 3) as an element contributing emotive force to a given passage. I do not mean to refute the notion of seriousness underlying Cortázar's usage of foreign words. In my judgement, however, the stylistic emphasis involved is light and humorous, not heavy and serious.

[21] I intend to clarify Cortázar's concept of what constitutes literary language in the course of my discussion.

conversation with La Maga, Oliveira suspects her of sleeping with
Gregorovius and informs her that he is willing to move out of the
apartment they share. Witness the following dialog:

> – No tenés por qué irte – dijo la Maga – ¿Hasta cuándo vas
> a seguir imaginando falsedades?
> – Imaginando falsedades – dijo Oliveira –. Hablás como en
> los diálogos de las mejores novelas rioplatenses. Ahora sola-
> mente te falta reírte con todas las vísceras de mi grotesquería
> sin pareja, y la rematás fenómeno. (100)

Note that Oliveira is not satisfied with criticizing La Maga's language. He takes advantage of the occasion to mimic the florid,
rhetorical literary language of some of his compatriots. In other
instances, when Oliveira's own language unintentionally waxes
literary, he is quick to censure it.

> Sí, te caés por un momento hacia adentro, hasta que las de-
> fensas de la vigilia, oh la bonita expresión, oh lenguaje, se
> encargan de detener. (408)

Elsewhere, Cortázar's criticism of the literary cliché becomes
more serious even though the playful tone is never entirely absent
from his work.[22] I refer to Chapter 34, the "Galdós chapter" in
which lines from Galdós' novel *Lo prohibido* alternate with those
of Oliveira's interior monolog.[23] Recall that La Maga has recently
disappeared and that Oliveira, already feeling the weight of her
absence while thinking about her, comes upon the Galdós novel
she had been reading. He begins to read and as the lines alternate,
his thoughts alternate between La Maga and a critique of the
prose he is reading. Consider some of his remarks about this
prose:

> . . . una novela, mal escrita . . . esta sopa fría y desabrida . . .
> una lengua hecha de frases preacuñadas para transmitir ideas
> archipodridas . . . . (227)

[22] Word games abound in *Rayuela*. Cortázar plays with language frequently –
almost obsessively – as did his Irish predecessor who expanded the frontiers of
the novel at the beginning of the twentieth century. In addition to the *hachismo*,
his favorite games are: *juegos en el cementerio* (270), *diálogos típicos* (279),
jitanjáforas (280), *preguntas-balanzas* (294), *ispamerikano* (345) and *glíglico* (428).
[23] J. S. Bernstein, "*Rayuela*, Chapter 34: A Structural Reading," *Hispanófila*,
No. 52 (September 1974), pp. 61–70.

After Galdós uses the word "lisonjero," Oliveira repeats the phrase in which it was used and then comments :

> Lisonjero, desde quién sabe cuándo no oía esa palabra, cómo se nos empobrece el lenguaje a los criollos, de chico yo tenía presentes muchas más palabras que ahora, leía esas mismas novelas, me adueñaba de un inmenso vocabulario perfectamente inútil por lo demás, *pulcro y distinguidísimo*, eso sí. (231)[24]

On the basis of these remarks, Cortázar's attitude toward Galdós' language is clear. No longer is the question one of a literary word, phrase, or expression that Cortázar singles out for criticism because of its worn-out and/or artificial nature. Now a whole manner of viewing and using language meets with Cortázar's criticism. This criticism should not be viewed, however, in light of any personal or individual attack. Here we see a situation not unlike that of Enrique González Martínez vis-à-vis Rubén Darío. Cortázar does not attack Galdós the man or even Galdós' language in itself. What he does offer is a critique of a tradition – the Realistic, the Descriptive – and he criticizes Galdós' language as representative of that tradition. Cortázar feels that one cannot express the reality of the twentieth-century human predicament within the framework of a nineteenth-century tradition, a language "hecha de frases preacuñadas para transmitir ideas archipodridas." Cortázar does not criticize Galdós; he criticizes the twentieth-century inheritors and imitators of Galdosian language.

What is the significance of this aversion to language, whether it be directed against the cliché (in speech or in literature) or against the high-sounding pomposity of literary language? Actually, Cortázar's preoccupation with language takes on a tone more strident than that of mere aversion; he explicitly declares himself to be the enemy of words and to be at war with them (99, 485). One of the *Morelliana* chapters (Chapter 112) offers an excellent indication of how this war is to be waged. Morelli tells how he is revising a narrative of his that he wishes to be as un-

[24] The italicized words, "*pulcro y distinguidísimo*," are from a sentence Oliveira had just read in the Galdós text: "Era entonces un señor menos viejo de lo que parecía, vestido siempre como los jóvenes elegantes, pulcro y distinguidísimo" (231).

literary as possible. He comes upon the clause: "Ramón emprendió el descenso . . .", which he crosses out and replaces with:
"Ramón empezó a bajar." He admits that the latter form is
rougher and more prosaic, but

> . . . lo que me repele en "emprendió el descenso" es el uso
> decorativo de un verbo y un sustantivo que no empleamos casi
> nunca en el habla corriente; en suma, me repele el lenguaje
> literario (en mi obra, se entiende). (538)

This decorative use of language, then, Morelli's former style
of writing, indicates to him somewhat of a departure from authenticity, from human concerns. He goes on to confess that the
results of his correcting processes really bore him. He realizes
that he writes "badly" now (he uses the verb "desescribir") and
claims that "ya no hay diálogo o encuentro con el lector, hay
solamente esperanza de un cierto diálogo con un cierto y remoto
lector" (539). This certain reader, of course, refers to the *lector-
cómplice,* who would have to empathize with Morelli's
(Cortázar's) preoccupations and concerns. Morelli proceeds to
clarify his point of view, his revulsion from literary language, by
affirming that his being repelled by it is actually due to the
changing scope of his preoccupations. Whereas before, Morelli's
decorative use of language was the reflection and result of predominantly esthetic concerns, he came to fear that "los órdenes
estéticos son más un espejo que un pasaje para la ansiedad meta-
física." Morelli identifies the change in tendency of his work as
advancing ever more toward an ethical level and away from the
esthetic (the parallel here to Cortázar's own work is obvious; see
2 and 3). His attitude towards his tools – words, language – is
a reflection of this changed attitude. This attitude to language is
also unmistakably the one advanced by Cortázar in his treatment
of Oliveira's metaphysical anxiety – an aversion to the purely
decorative or ornamental and an emphasis upon what is actually
used in current speech, ranging from the *voseo* and other speech
characteristics of the Río de la Plata area to a caricaturesque
portrayal of Spaniards' speech (the monologous nature of dialog
[279] and the ever present "coño" and "puñetero" whenever
Perico Romero speaks) to the more universally used scatological
characteristics of everyday speech.

In short, Oliveira-Morelli-Cortázar manifests a desire to employ authentic language, language actually used in current speech. Needless to say, different people will exhibit different speech characteristics and the educated language of the *Morelliana* must obviously be different from the lyric simplicity of La Maga's letter to Rocamadour ("Bebe Rocamadour, bebé bebé." [Ch. 32]). The clause "Ramón emprendió el descenso," however, is considered too artificial even for the literary man Morelli. The search for authenticity in language, as I have thus far described it, unquestionably shows a realistic tendency in Cortázar. It is important to note that this in no way signifies mere machine-like reproduction of plain speech, notwithstanding Cortázar's prowess with this technique (e. g. *Los premios,* 1960). Cortázar's attitudes toward language emphasize an authenticity devoid of false, pompous (literary) language and devoid of the tired phrase, the hackneyed expression, the cliché.

Purification through Language

So that even though, on the one hand, Morelli considers his present writing prosaic and impoverished, it becomes clear that his shift of emphasis from the esthetic to the ethical is actually a purification process. In Chapter 99, where the Club members discuss at length Morelli's attitudes to language, Oliveira summarizes as follows:

> En lo que acabás de leernos está bien claro que Morelli condena en el lenguaje el reflejo de una óptica y de un *Organum* falsos o incompletos, que nos enmascaran la realidad, la humanidad. A él en el fondo no le importa demasiado el lenguaje, salvo en el plano estético. Pero esa referencia al *ethos* es inequívoca. Morelli entiende que el mero escribir estético es un escamoteo y una mentira, que acaba por suscitar al lector-hembra, al tipo que no quiere problemas sino soluciones, o falsos problemas ajenos que le permiten sufrir cómodamente sentado en su sillón, sin comprometerse en el drama que también debería ser el suyo. (500)

On the basis of this insistence on the ethical plane of language and its identification with an authentic reality, it is not difficult to conclude that Morelli-Cortázar is a "committed" writer. He is

committed in that his principal concern is man and his reality
rather than purely esthetic categories. Etienne best indicates the
nature of this commitment when he points out differences between Morelli and the Surrealists: "Los surrealistas creyeron que
el verdadero lenguaje y la verdadera realidad estaban censurados
y relegados por la estructura racionalista y burguesa del occidente" (502). Etienne says that this was the basic premise of the
Surrealists and an accurate one. He goes on to say, though, that
the Surrealists became obsessed with this primary stage of the
problem and never progressed from there.

> Los surrealistas se colgaron de las palabras en vez de despegarse
> brutalmente de ellas, como quisiera hacer Morelli desde la
> palabra misma. Fanáticos del verbo en estado puro, pitonisos
> frenéticos, aceptaron cualquier cosa mientras no pareciera ex-
> cesivamente gramatical. No sospecharon bastante que la crea-
> ción de todo un lenguaje, aunque termine traicionando su
> sentido, muestra irrefutablemente la estructura humana, sea la
> de un chino o la de un piel roja. Lenguaje quiere decir residen-
> cia en una realidad, vivencia en una realidad. Aunque sea cierto
> que el lenguaje que usamos nos traiciona (y Morelli no es el
> único en gritarlo a todos los vientos) no basta con querer
> liberarlo de sus tabúes. Hay que re-vivirlo, no re-animarlo.
> (503)

In order to re-live language, suggests Gregorovius, one must have
a notion of the reality it is to reflect, of the human structure it is
to show: "No se puede revivir el lenguaje si no se empieza por
intuír de otra manera casi todo lo que constituye nuestra realidad.
Del ser al verbo, no del verbo al ser" (503). It seems reasonable
to assume that the ideas and attitudes about language advanced
by Oliveira, Morelli, and the Club members represent partial or
fragmentary aspects which, when taken as a whole, constitute
Cortázar's ideas on the subject.

We have already seen that Cortázar's principal concern is that
language be authentic in order to reflect an authentic reality.
What conceptions of reality are not authentic? For one, the reality of the post-war era dominated by emphasis upon science and
technology. Cortázar's attitude seems to be that technological
reality is inauthentic not because it is false in itself but because

it is partial and fragmentary – and therefore false (506-07). It is fragmentary because it excludes or relegates to inferior positions non-mechanical, non-causal categories such as Poetry and a poetic vision of the world. Etienne says: "Cuando leo a Morelli tengo la impresión de que busca una interacción menos mecánica, menos causal de los elementos que maneja . . ." (505). But a poetic reality would be equally fragmentary and false for the same reason, because it would exclude an essential segment of reality, the technological, which cannot be ignored by anyone who is even casually aware of his environment. Oliveira underscores these ideas in the following passage. The Club members had been discussing Morelli's desire to destroy literature and how they were to aid him in this task. Babs wonders about the end result of this destruction. Oliveira responds:

– Me pregunto – dijo Oliveira –. Hasta hace unos veinte años había la gran respuesta: la Poesía, ñata, la Poesía. Te tapaban la boca con la gran palabra. Visión poética del mundo, conquista de una realidad poética. Pero después de la última guerra, te habrás dado cuenta de que se acabó. Quedan poetas, nadie lo niega, pero no los lee nadie.
– No digas tonterías – dijo Perico –. Yo leo montones de versos.
– Claro, yo también. Pero no se trata de los versos, che, se trata de todo eso que anunciaban los surrealistas y que todo poeta desea y busca, la famosa realidad poética. Creeme, querido, desde el año cincuenta estamos en plena realidad tecnológica, por lo menos estadísticamente hablando. Muy mal, una lástima, habrá que mesarse los cabellos, pero es así. (504)

This dualistic concept of reality – science and technology on the one hand and poetry on the other – may also be identified in more generic terms as the dichotomy between reality and fantasy. As I stated in the chapter on "The Quest" and went on to qualify on the basis of an analysis of *Rayuela*'s structures (Ch. 2), Cortázar does not believe in this dualism. We have seen that he does not consider as authentic any vision of reality, be it scientific or poetic, Realistic or Fantastic, which by its very nature is exclusive, partial, and incomplete. Cortázar's vision of authentic reality, then, must necessarily encompass ideas of fusion and solution of traditionally non-fusible and insoluble aspects of life – the scientific with the poetic, the real with the fantastic, the horse with the unicorn.[25]

[25] See Mario Vargas Llosa, "Preguntas a Julio Cortázar," in *Cinco miradas sobre Cortázar* (Buenos Aires: Tiempo Contemporáneo, 1968), pp. 84–86. Cortázar here clearly affirms his belief in the indivisibility of life and of literature, and uses the words *caballo* and *unicornio* to refer to the realistic and fantastic tendencies in his work.

One may indeed arrive at an understanding of Cortázar's view of reality by examining the attitudes to language expressed in the novel, as I have attemped to show in the preceding chapter. But an examination of Cortázar's style – the manner in which he uses language – will serve to further illuminate the way in which he views reality as a harmonious fusion of customarily discordant categories. Interestingly enough, at one point in the novel, Morelli indicates the basic nature of this fusion in his own prose using a rather specialised vocabulary.

> Asisto hace años a los signos de podredumbre en mi escritura . . . Después de todo podrirse significa terminar con la impureza de los compuestos y devolver sus derechos al sodio, al magnesio, al carbono químicamente puros. Mi prosa se pudre sintáctica- mente y avanza – con tanto trabajo – hacia la simplicidad. (488)

On the level of content, it is easy to see how this passage points to the kind of fusion inherent in Cortázar's concept of reality. For here, decay and purification are fused and considered within the same context, not seen as discordant or cacophonous. On the level of form, a similar fusion occurs but in a different way. Morelli, describing his prose in terms of both decay and purifica- tion, is actually referring to a dimension of his prose which binary, dualistic logic would term "fantastic." Morelli and Cortázar consider this dimension, this kind of fantasy, to be the essence of authenticity. What is interesting to note, however, is that Morelli describes this fantastic (poetic) aspect of his prose within the framework of a chemical (scientific) vocabulary. The form re- flects the essence of the content – the fusive idea – in the above passage. And I have affirmed this idea to be fundamental to Cortázar's vision of reality. Now let us see how some significant stylistic aspects of the novel reflect this view.

There are two main stylistic characteristics of *Rayuela* which I shall call the additive and the elliptical. Both characteristics appear with great frequency and force throughout the novel (sometimes in the same sentence, as I shall illustrate below). The fact that these two stylistic features are basically heterogeneous, even opposites, and together form the most significant character- istic of Cortázar's style in *Rayuela,* reflects the fusive idea inherent in his vision of reality. The additive style consists of anaphora (the repetition of words at the beginning of successive clauses), other forms of repetition and reiteration, and different kinds of enumeration. The elliptical style may be defined essentially as a subtractive or omissive characteristic.

Additives

In an article which inspired my classification of this additive aspect of Cortázar's style, Leo Spitzer wrote that "todo rasgo de estilo es, en sí mismo, neutro; adquiere su particular eficacia solo por su enlace con tal o cual actitud particular."[26] The truth of this statement is certainly pertinent to the stylistic element under discussion. Additive and elliptical styles in themselves are not new, significant or noteworthy. They acquire significance in *Rayuela* from their coexistence and blending throughout the novel.

The simplest and most fundamental additive device is anaphora. Oliveira in Chapter 1:

> Sé que un día llegué a Paris, sé que estuve un tiempo vi- viendo de prestado, haciendo lo que otros hacen y viendo lo que otros ven. Sé que salías de un café de la rue du Cherche-Midi y que nos hablamos. (18)

This anaphora, "sé que," begins the fourth paragraph of the novel. It is especially effective considering the tone of the novel up to this point. Of the three previous paragraphs, two begin with questions and one with a negation:

> ¿Encontraría a la Maga? . . .
> Pero ella no estaría ahora en el puente. . . .
> ¿Qué venía yo a hacer al Pont des Arts?
> (15, 16)

In these first three paragraphs, expository in nature, Cortázar

26 "La enumeración caótica en la poesía moderna" (trans. Raimundo Lida), in his *Lingüística e historia literaria* (Madrid: Editorial Gredos, 1961), pp. 250–51.

begins *in medias res* by showing Oliveira searching for La Maga, revealing Oliveira's enchantment with her, and generally setting the atmosphere for what is to follow, that is, a man-woman relationship in Paris. The exposition up to this point, however, is still rather vague. The anaphora of the fourth paragraph introduces a positive brusqueness and intensity to the narrative. After the uncertain nature of the first three paragraphs, the "sé que" repetition adds a definitiveness to the narrative, the real beginning, the foundation for the remaining exposition. It also indicates the naturalness and rapidity with which Oliveira met La Maga.

Cortázar also utilizes a Biblical type of panegyrical anaphora, reminiscent of the form of the Sermon on the Mount.

Felices los que eligen, los que aceptan ser elegidos, los hermosos héroes, los hermosos santos, los escapistas perfectos. (34)

Feliz de ella que podía creer sin ver, que formaba cuerpo con la duración, el continuo de la vida. Feliz de ella que estaba dentro de la pieza, que tenía derecho de ciudad en todo lo que tocaba y convivía . . . . (35)

Felices los que vivían y dormían en la historia . . . . Felices los que amaban al prójimo como a sí mismos. (474-75)

In the first example above, the anaphoric "felices" becomes part of an enumeration, noteworthy for its energetic last item, which contributes surprise, irony, and a common characteristic for the previously enumerated items. In spite of the irony here, the anaphoric "felices" retains, nevertheless, its panegyrical nature. It is apparent from the context (Oliveira's lamenting his inability to be a man of action), that he admires greatly the "escapistas perfectos" to whom he refers. This attitude also forms the basis for my conclusions regarding the panegyrical anaphora in the second and third examples. The narrator genuinely seems to consider as happy those to whom he refers, that is the participants in life rather than mere spectators, though he definitely implies that their happiness has certain limitations which he himself has surpassed. The particular nature of the panegyrical anaphora "feliz," then, is due to the fact that it expresses both eulogy and irony.

Other types of reiterative devices abound in the novel. La

Maga's letter to Rocamadour in the country (Chapter 32), for example, consists of long, seemingly endless sentences whose most dominant punctuation is the vocative reiteration of the child's name throughout the entire letter-chapter. The effect is percussive and rhythmic, litany-like and magical, as if La Maga's reiterated incantation of the name Rocamadour reflected a desire to produce the actual presence of the child.

At times the repetition of a phrase or sentence will provide a bridge between chapters and announce a varied restatement of a particular theme (see 5, pp. 67-68). Chapter 6 describes the general state of relations between Oliveira and La Maga, and ends with the phrase: "Pero el amor, esa palabra . . .". Chapter 7 consists of a one-page, first-person description of Oliveira and La Maga making love. Chapter 8 returns to describe them going to look at the fish at the Quai de la Megisserie. Then, according to the second manner of reading the novel, the reader turns to Chapter 93, which begins with the same final words of Chapter 6: *"Pero el amor, esa palabra . . ."*. The rest of the chapter deals with the same love theme, here treated in a more comprehensive manner. Here Oliveira goes into an extended divagation on not only love but also language and literature. The repeated phrase serves to connect thematically the new chapter with the previous ones (6, 7, and 8) and, at the same time, to announce the varied restatement (now amplified and extended) of the love theme.

Cortázar uses a similar technique with the image "ríos metafísicos," which La Maga first utters to warn Oliveira against a type of metaphysical suicide that could be as fatal as the literal suicide she had been considering. Then he repeats the image in other parts of the novel, sometimes to evoke the memory of La Maga when Oliveira is away from her:

> *Hay ríos metafísicos.* Sí, querida, claro. Y vos estarás cuidando a tu hijo, llorando de a ratos, y aquí ya es otro día y un sol amarillo que no calienta. (114)

Elsewhere, Cortázar will interject the image in his narrative, rightly taking for granted the reader's familiarity with it and all it suggests (absence of passion, lifelessness). In the Berthe Trépat episode, for example, Oliveira tries to console her after the concert:

De golpe un gran sollozo la sacudió como si descargara un
acorde en el aire. "Y todo es lo de siempre . . .", alcanzó a
entender Oliveira, que luchaba en vano para evadir las sen-
saciones personales, para refugiarse en algún río metafísico,
naturalmente. (134)

And again in the same episode, but during the concert, Cortázar
uses the same image when describing Oliveira's growing sym-
pathy for Berthe Trépat:

De golpe comprobaba que todas sus reacciones derivaban de
una cierta simpatía por Berthe Trépat, a pesar de la *Pavana* y
de Rose Bob. "Hacía tiempo que no me pasaba esto," pensó.
"A ver si con los años me empiezo a ablandar." Tantos ríos
metafísicos y de golpe se sorprendía con ganas de ir al hospital
a visitar al viejo, o aplaudiendo a esa loca encorsetada. (130)

Then later on in the chapter, as Oliveira ushers the grotesque
Berthe through the streets of Paris, the image is again repeated
and combined with another:

"Si me llegan a ver Etienne o Wong se va a armar una del
demonio", pensaba Oliveira. Por qué tenía que importarle ya
lo que pensaran Etienne o Wong, como si después de los ríos
metafísicos mezclados con algodones sucios el futuro tuviese
alguna importancia. (139)

The "algodones sucios," of course, refers to the cotton with
which La Maga used to clean the infant Rocamadour. The
image as it is used here, however, refers to the entire experience
of Oliveira's sharing a room with La Maga and the child. From
the above examples, it is now easier to see what connotations are
expressed by the repeated image, "ríos metafísicos." It suggests
cool reflection, alienation, and lifelessness, all characteristics of
Oliveira with which he is not at all satisfied. The repetitions
seem to indicate his inability to shake off these characteristics.[27]

[27] Cortázar shows explicit concern with repetition in a more comprehensive
sense in Chapter 66, where the narrator mentions how Morelli would like to
draw certain ideas and describes the design in the margin of his notes:
"Repetición obsesiva de una espiral temblorosa . . ." (425). Also, one of the
many endings Morelli considers for his unfinished book consists of the repetition
of the sentence: "En el fondo sabía que no se puede ir más allá porque no lo
hay" (425). These remarks tend to associate repetition with qualities suggesting
failure, inconclusiveness, and openness (for remarks on openness in the novel,
see note 19).

Repetitions, then, to form a bridge between chapters, for variations on a theme, and to indicate certain unchanging qualities
of Oliveira are curiously combined in another instance. In Chapter 19 La Maga suggests that she and Oliveira live together.
Oliveira accepts, and the narrator describes his state of mind at
the time :

> . . . en ese momento le daba lo mismo vivir con la Maga o solo,
> andaba caviloso y la mala costumbre de rumiar largo cada cosa
> se le hacía cuesta arriba pero inevitable.   (97)

Here we see explicit mention of Oliveira's unchanging characteristics, his "ríos metafísicos." Then, true to form, Oliveira proceeds to reflect on problems of finding a center, unity, plurality,
and language (98, 99). At the beginning of the following chapter
(Chapter 90), according to the second way, we read the same
sentence as the one above, with one change.

> En *esos días* [italics mine][28] andaba caviloso, y la mala
> costumbre de rumiar largo cada cosa se le hacía cuesta arriba
> pero inevitable.   (473)

The narrator then proceeds to the topics of Oliveira's meditations,
principally "la encrucijada en que se sentía metido" (473). In
this Chapter 90 the reader still sees Oliveira seeking a center, as
in Chapter 19, where the sentence to be repeated first appears.
But the subjects treated in Chapter 90 – action and passivity,
rather than unity and plurality – are variations on the sole theme
of Oliveira's seeking a center to his life. So the repetition of the
sentence here provides the bridge with Chapter 19 and announces
the theme variation to follow.

Enumeration, unlike repetition or reiteration which consists of
the same word or words repeated, involves different words which
have, nevertheless, a complementary semantic value. Scholars
have classified and analyzed enumerative techniques according
to two main categories: regular or homogeneous enumeration

---

[28] Notice how the minor change to "esos días" from "ese momento" of the
original utterance is a preparation for the opening-out and the variations of
the theme which follow.

and chaotic or heterogeneous enumeration.[29] They have further classified the results of their studies of individual writers by applying the terms "conjunctive" or "disjunctive" depending on the type of enumeration expressed. Amado Alonso, for example, shows how Neruda's enumerative style is primarily disjunctive: that is, the effect of Neruda's heterogeneous enumerations is the expression of the fragmented and disintegrated state of the world. Schumann and Spitzer, on the other hand, point to the conjunctive effect of Whitman's chaotic enumerations as a reflection of his pantheistic vision of the world. In his study of enumerative technique in Peruvian narrators, Núñez states that the incidence of chaotic enumeration reaches its apogee in the poetic prose of César Vallejo and his contemporaries, while more recent prose, such as that of José María Arguedas and Mario Vargas Llosa, reveals the absence of chaotic enumeration. He attributes this to a new sense of prose fiction which tends to be more direct, ". . . eludiendo forzadas asociaciones de imágenes o ideas, metáforas complicadas o lirismos envolventes" (Núñez, p. 338). He concludes that chaotic enumeration

> . . . es recurso o rasgo de estilo de la poesía, y en ella anida y se hace consustancial, mientras en la prosa es modalidad fugaz, pasajera, aunque indudablemente vital y, en ciertos momentos de crisis, necesaria. (Núñez, p. 339)

Characteristics of both these stages are present in *Rayuela*. Cortázar's novel contains both poetic prose, as in the following enumeration:

> Nos arde un fuego inventado, una incandescente tura,[30] un artilugio de la raza, una ciudad que es el Gran Tornillo, la

[29] In addition to the Spitzer article already cited (note 26), see Detlev W. Schumann, "Enumerative Style and its Significance in Whitman, Rilke, Werfel," *Modern Language Quarterly*, III (1942), 171–204; Amado Alonso, "Disjecta membra y objetos heterogéneos," in his *Poesía y estilo de Pablo Neruda*, 3rd ed. (Buenos Aires: Losada, 1966), pp. 312–26; Estuardo Núñez, "La enumeración caótica en la narrativa peruana contemporánea," XIII Congreso Internacional de Literatura Iberoamericana, *La novela iberoamericana contemporánea* (Caracas: Organización de Bienestar Estudiantil, Universidad Central, 1968), pp. 321–39.

[30] A sentence on the previous page supplies an explanation for the use of the suffix "tura" in the passage cited: "Nuestra verdad posible tiene que ser *invención*, es decir escritura, literatura, pintura, escultura, agricultura, piscicultura, todas las turas de este mundo" (439).

horrible aguja con su ojo nocturno por donde corre el hilo del
Sena, máquina de torturas como puntillas, agonía en una jaula
atestada de golondrinas enfurecidas. (140)

and a more direct, down-to-earth, colloquial approach, such as I
have already indicated. Cortázar uses many forms of enumeration
throughout the novel. There is the regular or homogeneous variety, as in the following description of the clocharde Emmanuèle:

> Sobre un fondo indescifrable donde se acumularían camisones
> pegados a la piel, blusas regaladas y algún corpiño capaz de
> contener unos senos ominosos, se iban sumando, dos, tres, quizá
> cuatro vestidos, el guardarropas completo, y por encima un saco
> de hombre con una manga casi arrancada, una bufanda soste-
> nida por un broche de latón con una piedra verde y otra roja,
> y en el pelo increíblemente teñido de rubio una especie de
> vincha verde de gasa, colgando de un lado. (528)

The effect here is literally accumulative – an enumerated series of
descriptive phrases to indicate the enormous accumulation of
clothing on Emmanuèle. This is definitely conjunctive enumeration. But the above example would have to be considered a com-
plex enumeration, since to the simple enumeration of articles of
clothing are added such items as "y por encima" and "y en el
pelo increíblemente teñido de rubio." These words technically
are intruders in the enumerative series, but do not seem to detract,
in this case, from the rapidity and effectiveness of the enumeration.

A simple enumeration of the homogeneous sort may be seen in
the following reference to Oliveira and La Maga's love-making
in different hotel rooms: "Se acostumbraron a comparar los
acolchados, las puertas, las lámparas, las cortinas . . ." (43). This
is simply a rapid and efficient way to enrich the experience
described.

Chaotic enumeration is a constant stylistic feature of *Rayuela*.
Consider the particular effectiveness of such a technique when
Oliveira relates his first impression of Paris:

> Aquí había sido primero como una sangría, un vapuleo de
> uso interno, una necesidad de sentir el estúpido pasaporte de
> tapas azules en el bolsillo del saco, la llave del hotel bien segura

en el clavo del tablero. El miedo, la ignorancia, el deslumbra-
miento: Esto se llama así, eso se pide así, ahora esa mujer va a
sonreír, más allá de esa calle empieza el Jardin des Plantes. (24)

This kind of enumeration adds more than rapid, dynamic effects
of expression; the enumerative chaos is actually a reflection of the
chaos experienced by Oliveira during his first moments in Paris.

It is not possible, however, to reduce the great variety of enumerative techniques employed by Cortázar to a simple classification of regular or chaotic, conjunctive or disjunctive. Consider
the following description of Morelli's accident:

> Las opiniones eran que el viejo se había resbalado, que el
> auto había "quemado" la luz roja, que el viejo había querido
> suicidarse, que todo estaba cada vez peor en París, que el trá-
> fico era monstruoso, que el viejo no tenía la culpa, que el viejo
> tenía la culpa, que los frenos del auto no andaban bien, que
> el viejo era de una imprudencia temeraria, que la vida estaba
> cada vez más cara, que en París había demasiados extranjeros
> que no entendían las leyes del tráfico y les quitaban el trabajo
> a los franceses. (118)

There is no doubt that the items in the enumeration contradict
each other, but to term this a chaotic enumeration with all the
implications of such a label (reflection of the author's vision of a
chaotic world) would not be accurate. The effect of such an enumeration (the variety of eye-witness accounts) seems to be predominantly humorous. It is difficult to see how this kind of stylistic element, technically within the definition of chaotic enumeration, could possibly correspond to "la inquietud del hombre de
nuestra época, el cual pertenece a una sociedad convulsionada,
industrial y pluralista, vibrante, insegura, en transición" (Núñez,
p. 321).

Even though the enumerations in *Rayuela* do not lend themselves to easy classifications, their frequent and conspicuous presence makes them a significant aspect of Cortázar's additive
style. And as a stylistic technique, enumeration ties in with
Cortázar's ideas and attitudes about language and reality. Etienne,
in a parenthetical expression, provides a clue as to the nature of
this relationship between enumeration and reality. The Club
members have been discussing their ideas about true reality.

Oliveira suggests the term Yonder. Etienne then insists on the present-tense character of this Yonder:

> Lo que llamamos realidad, la verdadera realidad que también llamamos Yonder (a veces ayuda darle muchos nombres a una entrevisión, por lo menos se evita que la noción se cierre y se acartone), esa verdadera realidad, repito, no es algo por venir, una meta, el último peldaño, el final de una evolución. (508)

The statement within the parenthesis serves to show the significance of the omnipresent enumerations ("muchos nombres"). We have already seen how Morelli feels himself to be at war with words, "las proxenetas relucientes" (150). Words, "los supuestos instrumentos cognoscitivos" (558), diminish and betray reality (558). But this presents a problem for the novelist, for whom words serve as his only tools.[31] Cortázar's "entrevisión" of reality, Yonder, "lo otro" which is reflected in his novel, then, will find expression by means of "las perras palabras" (149-50), which quite frequently are arranged in an enumerative manner. Enumeration, as used by Cortázar, is a stylistic characteristic which effectively avoids petrification of his "entrevisión."

Ellipses

The second predominant stylistic technique in *Rayuela,* elliptical style, is virtually an opposite of additive style. Cortázar's elliptical style is characterized by linguistic elements (words, phrases, entire sentences) that are missing from his prose.[32] While it is true that *Rayuela*'s elliptical style is not as conspicuous as additive style, it is just as frequent and is just as integral a part of the novel.

Consider, first, instances of absence in combination with repetition. At the beginning of the novel, Oliveira refers to Madame Léonie:

[31] The idea that words falsify experience by solidifying and immobilizing it but are nonetheless necessary in order to suggest the profound reality intuited by the true poet is an integral part of the philosophy of Henri Bergson. Raimundo Lida has demonstrated this masterfully in his "Bergson, filósofo del lenguaje," in *Letras hispánicas* (México: Fondo de Cultura Económica, 1958), pp. 45-99.

[32] Morelli himself suggests the importance of this elliptical aspect of the novel in the one-sentence Chapter 137: "Si el volumen o el tono de la obra pueden llevar a creer que el autor intentó una suma, apresurarse a señalarle que está ante la tentativa contraria, la de una *resta* implacable" (595).

¿Qué venía yo a hacer al Pont des Arts? Me parece que ese jueves de diciembre tenía pensado cruzar a la orilla derecha y beber vino en el cafecito de la rue des Lombards donde madame Léonie me mira la palma de la mano y me anuncia viajes y sorpresas. Nunca te llevé a que madame Léonie te mirara la palma de la mano, a lo mejor tuve miedo de que leyera en tu mano alguna verdad sobre mí . . . . (16-17)

And then soon afterwards:

De manera que nunca te llevé a que madame Léonie, Maga; y sé . . . . (17)

Notice here the absence or omission of the verb "mirar" and the rest of the dependent clause. By itself, the above sentence with the omitted verb would be puzzling, its meaning obscure. Owing to the fact that the sentence is almost a repetition, however, its meaning is clear. The verb "mirar" and its object are not necessary. Actual speech or thought (rather than fictional narrative) is characterized by similar interruptions. In this particular case, there is a definite additive-ellipsis relationship. Our understanding of the elliptical statement depends on its repeated quality.

Another instance involving a combination of absence and repetition may be seen in the example below. In this case, the example under consideration takes the form of a literally elliptical sentence. See what happens with the image, "la fina raya":

Así es cómo alguien, sin saberlo, llega a mostrarte irrefutablemente un camino que por su parte sería incapaz de seguir. La Maga no sabrá nunca cómo su dedo apuntaba hacia la fina raya que triza el espejo, hasta qué punto ciertos silencios, ciertas atenciones absurdas, ciertas carreras de ciempiés deslumbrado eran el santo y seña para mi bien plantado estar en mí mismo, que no era estar en ninguna parte. En fin, eso de la fina raya . . . Si quieres ser feliz como me dices / No poetices, Horacio, no poetices. (499)

The elliptical statement here lacks a predicate and object, and the subject, "la fina raya," consists of a repetition as in the previous example cited. But this additive-ellipsis combination is different in that our comprehension of the elliptical statement depends not merely on what preceded it (the original expression of "la fina raya") but also on what follows (the couplet). Oliveira uses the couplet to criticize the serious, explanatory tendency of his language. Here it also serves to clarify the ellipsis.

Though it may seem contradictory or at least unusual to proceed with an analysis of the presence of absence in a literary text, the reader who is acquainted with Cortázar's tendency to reduce and dissolve opposites will not merely discount any unusual qualification regarding a presence-absence relationship but will even strongly suspect and await its stylistic manifestations. Cortázar's concern with absence is conscious. Morelli remarks to Oliveira: "Me hubiera gustado entender mejor a Mallarmé, su sentido de la ausencia y del silencio era mucho más que un recurso extremo, un *impasse* metafísico" (625).[33] At another point in the novel, the reader discovers another dimension of the realistic nature of Morelli as a writer. We are told that Morelli tried to justify his narrative incoherencies by pointing out how they were but a reflection of reality.

> . . . la vida de los otros, tal como nos llega en la llamada realidad, no es cine sino fotografía, es decir que no podemos aprehender la acción sino tan solo sus fragmentos eleáticamente recortados. . . .
> Los puentes entre una y otra instancia de esas vidas tan vagas y poco caracterizadas, debería presumirlos o inventarlos el lector. . . . Pero a veces las líneas ausentes eran las más importantes, las únicas que realmente contaban. (532-33)

It is obvious, then, that the above examples indicate Morelli's belief in the importance of absence. And it is logical to assume that this idea would be reflected in Cortázar's style. We have examined instances of absence (ellipsis) in combination with its opposite, additives. Now let us consider how it works by itself.

A common characteristic in the novel, as we have seen, is the use of absence or ellipsis to produce the effect of a conversational tone, as in the example below concerning the sugar cube incident at the beginning of the novel:

[33] Recall Mallarmé's idea that the perfect poem was the one suggested by the blank sheet of paper. Once the first word was written, the poet then had to work with ever-narrowing possibilities of expression and ever-increasing limitations.

Y todo el mundo enfurecido, hasta yo con el azúcar apretado en la palma de la mano y sintiendo cómo se mezclaba con el sudor de la piel, cómo asquerosamente se deshacía en una especie de venganza pegajosa, esa clase de episodios todos los días. (23)

But the omission of verbs between noun and adjective of the first phrase and between noun and adverb of the last phrase does more than establish a conversational tone for the narrative; it also has the effect of indicating a concern, on the part of the narrator, with a rapid presentation of the essentials of the particular situation evoked.

Conversational tone and essentials of a given situation are also achieved not just by the omission of a verb or two but by whole sections of sentences. Consider the following passage (italics mine):

Y entonces en esos días íbamos a los cine-clubs a ver películas mudas, *porque yo con mi cultura,* no es cierto, y vos pobrecita no entendías absolutamente nada de esa estridencia amarilla convulsa previa a tu nacimiento, esa emulsión estriada donde corrían los muertos; pero de repente pasaba por ahí Harold Lloyd y entonces te sacudías el agua del sueño y al final te convencías de que todo había estado muy bien, *y que Pabst y que Fritz Lang.* (18-19)

Here, Cortázar uses the elliptical phrases as direction-indicators, that is, to point out the particular direction or gist of a conversation rather than to record it in faithful detail.

An elliptical and an oblique style combine to provide a forceful, intense expression of emotion (Oliveira's weeping) at the end of the Berthe Trépat episode. Recall how Oliveira, feeling sorry for Berthe, had accompanied her home, only to be ultimately accused by the pitiful old lady of attempting to seduce her. After she slaps him and begins to cause a commotion, the scene shifts to the street, where we see a stunned Oliveira weeping. But observe the manner in which this is described:

En la esquina de la rue Tournefort, Oliveira se dio cuenta de que llevaba todavía el cigarrillo entre los dedos, apagado por la lluvia y medio deshecho. Apoyándose contra un farol, levantó

la cara y dejó que la lluvia lo empapara del todo. Así nadie
podría darse cuenta, con la cara cubierta de agua nadie podría
darse cuenta. . . .
De cuando en cuando levantaba la mano y se la pasaba por la
cara, pero al final dejó que le lloviera, a veces sacaba el labio y
bebía algo salado que le corría por la piel. (149)

What is absent here is the direct expression of Oliveira's weeping. The verb "llorar" is not even mentioned. The scene is presented obliquely, with subtlety; this manner of presentation contributes a greater force and poignancy to the episode than would
be possible with a more direct, straightforward expression.

In conclusion, I have attempted to clarify in this analysis
Cortázar's aversion to language that is exclusively decorative and
ornamental and his desire to create a more authentic literary language by incorporating the most vital aspects of oral tradition
into his prose, thereby adding a more human dimension to his
novel. This human dimension does not consist merely of faithful
imitation of oral style but rather of a literary language which
carries a spontaneity similar to that of current speech (see 6).
The result is the fusion of a spoken style into and with a written
style. The additive and elliptical aspects of Cortázar's language
are predominantly characteristics of oral expression, yet together
form one of the principal foundations for his literary style.
Rapidity, immediacy, and, most important, spontaneity are all
characteristics which Cortázar's additive-elliptical style contributes to his prose, thereby intensifying and enriching its expres-
sive quality.

5 Conclusion

In the chapter on "The Quest" I attempted to explain, clarify, and comment on the philosophical and literary foundations on which the novel is based. Julio Cortázar in *Rayuela* depicts a man, Horacio Oliveira, who recognizes his existence to be empty and sterile because it lacks adequate affective quality. He wanders through Paris, which takes on the symbolic dimensions of a hopscotch chart, seeking to arrive at the "cielo." On a human level this Heaven portion corresponds to an absolute, a centre: meaningfulness and authenticity of life. Oliveira approaches authenticity in his love relationship with La Maga, whose spontaneous and natural personality and character are distinctly different from Oliveira's. But the love relationship does not last. Oliveira does not even realize his love for her until she disappears. Incapable of fully accepting her love in Paris, he came to look upon La Maga more as if she were a judge or witness who, by her very presence, would remind him of everything he lacked. In Buenos Aires Oliveira's actions seemed to indicate certain positive evidence regarding La Maga's influence on him. In the end, however, the awareness of his loss proves to be overpowering for Oliveira. Talita becomes La Maga; his friend Traveler becomes a mortal enemy. Oliveira breaks down and his quest fails.

Oliveira's quest is for authenticity of life; Morelli seeks an authenticity of expression. Morelli advances the idea of anti-literature, based on the destruction of such formulaic devices as traditionally ordered time and space and the moving forward of fictional narrative by cause-and-effect situations and characterizations. The anti-novel, according to Morelli, will suggest and stimulate other orders which will be perceived by the active reader. In order to evaluate Morelli's quest we must look to Cortázar. Morelli speculates and theorizes; Cortázar novelizes. Cortázar does put some of Morelli's ideas into practice. I pointed out how Oliveira, the Club members, and we ourselves may be characterized as accomplice readers of Morelli, for example. But Cortázar in *Rayuela* (practice) is not as radical as is Morelli in his notes (theory). Traditional means of expression (plot, characterizations) are not absent in *Rayuela*.

There are, nevertheless, certain subtle characteristics of the novel which, once perceived, serve to illuminate Cortázar's vision of life and literature contained therein and reveal *Rayuela*'s remarkable unity. The most apparent of these characteristics is the parallel or analogous nature of the quest undertaken by Oliveira in life and Morelli in literature. Both feel oppressed by forms of custom and tradition from which they seek release and, as a consequence, authenticity. Oliveira as a reflective man is limited by the tradition of dualistic thought which he feels to be a major cause of his spiritual poverty. He recognizes, laments, and unsuccessfully strives to correct his dehumanized condition. Morelli as a literary man reacts against the tradition of worn-out, ineffective literary intentions and forms.

If Oliveira fails and Morelli fails to exemplify, where is one to seek the unity of the novel? In their failure? Certainly not. The unity is to be found in Cortázar's expression, in the patterns of structure, language, and style I explored in Chapters 2, 3, and 4 of this study. The preoccupations and quest of Oliveira and Morelli form the principal theme of the novel. It is reasonable to assume, on the basis of what Cortázar himself has said in the novel and elsewhere and what critics of the novel have recognized, that Oliveira and Morelli together reflect the presence and vision of Cortázar. On this basis, Cortázar views life and literature as impoverished by fragmentation, by partial and incomplete notions of reality. In the metaphysical realm, this is expressed by Oliveira's attempt to escape the tradition of mind over sense. On the literary level, Morelli attempts to escape the tradition of ordered time, space, and form. The authenticity sought by Oliveira-Morelli-Cortázar seems to involve completion and integration in the greatest degree possible. Nowhere is this more evident than in the structural and stylistic features of *Rayuela,* which constitute a realization of what Oliveira and Morelli were only able to hope for.

The structural patterns of twos and threes analyzed in Chapter 2 reflect a fusive vision. Cortázar indicates the coming together of parts in his structuring of the sets of doubles (personages, past and present, Buenos Aires and Paris). He displays this integrative tendency even more forcefully by showing the interconnections between dissimilarities and by suggesting the "analogous consciousness" necessary to perceive the affinities. The expression of the affinities amongst heterogeneous categories indeed may be interpreted as a vision of the fluid reality sought by Oliveira-Morelli-Cortázar. But on the basis of this expression of the metaphoric or imagistic dimensions of life, one arrives at the ultimate conclusion that Julio Cortázar in *Rayuela* presents a poetic vision of reality.

This judgement alone is unsatisfactory, however, not because of inaccuracy or insignificance but rather because of its partial, fragmentary nature. The vision is yet incomplete. My Chapter 3 explored the ethical basis underlying Cortázar's consciousness of language. Analyzed in Chapter 4 was the infusion of spontaneity in the novel through categories of oral expression (additive-elliptical style). On this basis we may conclude that Cortázar offers a vitalized vision of literature.

The poetization of life and the vitalization of literature form the essence and unity of the novel. Julio Cortázar in *Rayuela* achieves the authenticity unsuccessfully sought by Oliveira and only postulated by Morelli.

Select bibliography

1 Paley de Francescato, Marta, "Bibliografía de y sobre Julio Cortázar," *Revista Iberoamericana*, XXXIX, Nos. 84-85 (julio-diciembre 1973), 697-726. The most complete bibliography compiled to date.

GENERAL STUDIES AND LITERARY HISTORY

2 Harss, Luis and Barbara Dohmann, "Julio Cortázar, or the Slap in the Face," in *Into the Mainstream : Conversations with Latin-American Writers,* New York : Harper and Row, 1966, pp. 206-45. The best all-around introduction to the man and his work.

3 Leal, Luis, "Situación de Julio Cortázar," *Revista Iberoamericana*, XXXIX, Nos. 84-85 (julio-diciembre 1973), 399-409. Places Cortázar within the context of contemporary Spanish American narrative and traces his literary trajectory.

CRITICAL STUDIES AND INTERVIEWS :

4 Barrenechea, Ana María, "La estructura de *Rayuela,* de Julio Cortázar," in *Litterae Hispanae et Lusitanae,* ed. Hans Flasche, München : Max Hueber Verlag, 1968, pp. 69-84; reprinted in *Nueva novela latinoamericana* II, ed. Jorge Lafforgue, Buenos Aires : Editorial Paidós, 1972, pp. 222-47. The best comprehensive study of *Rayuela*'s structure.

5 Boldori, Rosa, "Sentido y trascendencia de la estructura de *Rayuela,*" *Boletín de Literaturas Hispánicas* (Universidad del Litoral), No. 6 (1966), 59-69. A solid study, especially good on the ways in which Cortázar unifies seemingly unconnected chapters.

6 Donni de Mirande, Nelly, "Notas sobre la lengua de Cortázar," *Boletín de Literaturas Hispánicas* (Universidad del Litoral), No. 6 (1966), 71-83. A detailed discussion of Cortázar's approach to language in *Los premios* and *Rayuela*.

7 García Flores, Margarita, "Siete respuestas de Julio Cortázar," *Revista de la Universidad de México*, XXI, No. 7 (marzo 1967), 10-13. One of the most revealing interviews to appear, especially with regard to *Rayuela*.

8 Loveluck, Juan, "Aproximación a *Rayuela,*" *Revista Iberoamericana*, XXXIV, No. 65 (enero-abril 1968), 83-93. Particularly interesting for its examination of the "threeness" aspect of *Rayuela*.

9 Sola, Graciela de, *Cortázar y el hombre nuevo,* Buenos Aires : Editorial Sudamericana, 1968. One of the best studies of Cortázar's work as a whole, with special emphasis on *Rayuela*, its poetic qualities and ethical implications.

10 Sosnowski, Saúl, *Julio Cortázar : una búsqueda mítica,* Buenos Aires : Ediciones Noé, 1973. A well-documented study of Cortázar's narrative theory, his mythic vision, and their relation to modern thought; contains an excellent bibliography.